Henry Phelps Johnston

Observations on Judge Jones' loyalist history of the

American revolution.

How far is it an authority ..

Henry Phelps Johnston

Observations on Judge Jones' loyalist history of the American revolution.
How far is it an authority ..

ISBN/EAN: 9783337716073

Printed in Europe, USA, Canada, Australia, Japan

Cover: Foto ©ninafisch / pixelio.de

More available books at **www.hansebooks.com**

OBSERVATIONS

ON

JUDGE JONES' LOYALIST HISTORY

OF THE

AMERICAN REVOLUTION.

HOW FAR IS IT AN AUTHORITY?

" Facts speak louder than words."
JUDGE JONES

BY

HENRY P. JOHNSTON.

NEW YORK:

D. APPLETON & CO.

1880

INTRODUCTORY NOTE.

The recently published History of the American Revolution, by the contemporary loyalist Judge Thomas Jones, of New York,¹ contains statements which seem to call for criticism and refutation.

The propriety of noticing them may possibly be recognized in the fact that the work not only assumes to be an authority and has already been quoted as such, but some of the errors themselves have been repeated and are likely to be perpetuated by American historical writers.

The following pages are devoted mainly to a comparison of these statements with the correct record and such inferences as the comparison appears to authorize. Incidentally the question is considered whether the number and nature of the errors are not sufficient to affect the trustworthiness of the Judge's work, as an original source of information. In any view it is due to our Revolutionary history to examine unfriendly accounts with some care, especially where, as in the present case, they reverse accepted versions of events and transactions or make discreditable disclosures.

NEW YORK CITY, June 1, 1880.

History of New York during the Revolutionary War, and of the Leading Events in the Other Colonies at that Period. By Thomas Jones, Justice of the Supreme Court of the Province. Edited by Edward Floyd de Lancey. With Notes, Contemporary Documents, Maps, and Portraits. 2 vols. Printed for the New York Historical Society, New York, 1879.

1

CONTENTS.

OBSERVATIONS

ON

JUDGE JONES' LOYALIST HISTORY.

I.—JUDGE JONES' STANDING AS A WITNESS.

THERE are certain features of this History—noticeable and more or less important features—which ought properly to be had in mind in the course of examining the particular statements proposed.

The Judge's work, it will be observed, even upon the most superficial reading, proves to be a sweeping arraignment of the Revolution. The title of " History" applied to it might be regarded, indeed, as a misnomer, if in its use we are to understand that the Judge presents a candid and temperate account of the events of that period. Upon the minds of some of its readers, certainly, a contrary impression is produced. The work conveys and confirms the impression that purely historical illustration or reflection is not so much the author's object, as to treat of the movement for the purpose of condemning it—that it is much less a literary effort than an *ex-parte* case, a complaint, or a grand indictment of the train of events which resulted in American independence.

Perhaps a history of a different character could not have been expected from the Judge or from any one circumstanced as he was. In view of his political connections, his sympathies and temperament, it is not surprising that he should have vigorously resisted the claims of the Colonists.

Judge Jones, as we gather from his own representations, was one of the more prominent loyalists or tories of the time.

Living affluently at Great Neck. Long Island, possessed also of a large estate in New York, and related by marriage and social ties to few who were not as firm loyalists as himself, he may be regarded as the type of the American subject whose influence King George imagined would be strong enough to keep at least the province of New York from drifting into revolt. From 1769 to 1773 he had been Recorder of the city, when he was appointed to succeed his father as one of the justices of the Supreme Court of the Colony, a position in the gift of the royal governor. His associations, his office, his conservative mold, combined to determine his relations to the Revolution. There was nothing in its spirit or aim that he could approve. He looked upon it as at best a groundless, radical, and desperate movement to be treated with contempt, denounced or avoided. In his work he is unreserved in the avowal of his sentiments, and repeatedly declares his fidelity to the Crown and the Church of England, while he also shows himself a thoroughly good hater of agitation and republicanism. How far he publicly gave vent to his feelings and views does not appear, but at heart he was clearly neither neutral nor moderate, but uncompromising, and, judging from some of his own expressions, even virulent; and when subsequently he prepared a so-called history of the struggle, it was inevitably tinctured with the convictions, prejudices, and antipathies formed during its progress. The Judge necessarily wrote from a strictly partisan stand-point.

Judge Jones, furthermore, wrote under the pressure of bitter personal recollections. His own experiences during the war harmonizing little with his previous mode of life tended to exasperate his apparently sensitive, if not irritable, nature. Being charged, in the summer of 1776, when hostilities opened on Long Island, with disaffection to the American cause, he was arrested and removed to Connecticut, where he remained until released on parole in December following. Seized again as a prisoner in 1779, he was held several months longer, and finally exchanged in the spring of 1780. Nor were matters on his own side satisfactory. British commissaries and generals failed to treat him with due respect. He was pleased with few of the many civil and military appointments made either by the ministry at home or commanding officers in New York. Movements in the field should have been the reverse of or different from what they were, the Judge's criticisms, however, being made after their failure ; and the leaders, both civil and military, who were entrusted with the responsibility of crushing the rebellion deserved only a merciless handling for their non-success. The close of the war found his judicial position snatched from him, his property confiscated, and himself a refugee in England -conditions not favorable for a perfectly impartial treatment of events which affected him so disastrously.

A third noticeable feature of the work is the absence, with a few exceptions, of any authority, on the part of the Judge, for his many unlooked-for and remarkable statements. The reader is informed in the preface to the History that it gives "the account, observations, and comments of an eye-witness of acute intelligence, who was in a position, official and social, to know perfectly the events he was describing, and the parties and persons who took part therein on all sides." This responsible authorship should entitle it, *prima facie*, to every consideration. But it is pertinent to inquire how far it was possible for the Judge to be an eye-witness of what he describes. So far as current military events were concerned, he could have known personally very little about them. It can be shown that important movements occurred in and around New York, the details and objects of which he assumed to be acquainted with, but with which it appears he was not. There is no line drawn between facts coming and those not coming within his own observation. In addition, the Judge remained under the obligations of a strict military parole during nearly the entire, if not the entire, time from 1776 until he sailed for England in 1781. He had given his promise to Governor Trumbull, of Connecticut, to hold no "inimical correspondence with the enemy" after his return to his home, but "to conduct peaceably and quietly with respect to the present contest and troubles." As the Judge claims to have faithfully observed his parole, living at his residence, he was obviously debarred from witnessing anything important in the shape of "events." Clearly, too, he had very little if any intercourse with the British headquarters at New York where it might have been possible for him to obtain a certain amount of authentic intelligence. His severe and re-

peated strictures upon Generals Howe, Clinton, Robertson, and
other officers are not indicative of any familiarity in that direction. It can hardly be questioned, on the contrary, especially
as the Judge does not make the claim himself of being an "eye-
witness," that his knowledge of passing military transactions
was derived almost exclusively from third parties, from hearsay
or common rumor, from such meagre accounts as appeared in
the newspapers of the time, from official letters which were occasionally published, and possibly from the few narratives of the
war that had been printed before his death in 1793. These
sources of information do not entitle him to any special or superior consideration as an authority. What he obtained from
printed matter is not new, and what he learned from others is
only valuable as second-hand material which may or may not
have been true.

As to matters not military, on the other hand, but more of a
political or personal nature, the Judge ought presumably to
have had a considerable knowledge. But even here the value
of his statements, and more especially of his opinions and inferences, is to be tested by those common rules which the Judge
was doubtless in the habit of applying himself in determining
the credibility of a witness. Was he interested or prejudiced,
and if so, to what extent? and what his relations to the men and
events he criticises or condemns? Undoubtedly the Judge was
in a position to see and hear much, before the outbreak of the
war at least; but in what light, through what medium, in what
disposition of mind, did he see and hear and write? The Judge
seems to answer for himself--he was on the other side, a disappointed tory, a monarchist, a hater of revolutions, the American revolution in particular and of all who contributed to its
success. In this light he evidently cannot be regarded as an
unbiased witness. How far he was a valuable one may possibly
be shown.

In referring to these features of Judge Jones' work no reflection is cast upon his own political status. We must allow
him the right to choose the side he preferred. He was a tory,
a loyalist, and a loyalist by nature and inclination, as many
others were both in the city and province of New York. In
his history, which he wrote in England soon after the war, he
not only attacks the American cause, but the unsuccessful

British leaders as well; certain tories also are held up to the general scorn. What he presents is much of it novel and unexpected the narrative being at intervals a combination of assumed fact and argument—and his work will hereafter doubtless be consulted with a curious interest. But to consult it as a guide is another matter. In view of the characteristics just noticed no candid reader could be willing to accept the Judge unreservedly as an "authority," especially where he treats of his enemies, the revolutionary or whig party. The conviction remains that what he says of a damaging nature respecting them needs confirmation. Can a writer, it may be asked, command implicit confidence who is known to have been a thorough partisan, who appears to have undertaken his work for the purpose of putting certain men and transactions in an odious light before posterity, who indulges in extraordinary statements without hinting at the proof on which they stand, and whose personal experiences embittered him against those of whom he writes? The Judge is put forward as a contemporary and eye-witness, but the effect of this claim is seriously impaired when, he is also found approaching his subject, as he does, in *an intensely hostile attitude.*

If, from this, it sufficiently appears that upon general principles Judge Jones' standing as a witness and an authority is impeachable, there is good ground at the outset for going further and looking into some of the details of his testimony.

II.—THE JUDGE'S REVIEW OF HIS OWN CASE.

One of the first and most striking points inviting notice is the free and deliberate manner in which the Judge deals with persons and personal characters. Whatever may be said in general of his criticisms and alleged exposures, in certain instances they are so obviously libellous that it is much to be doubted whether he would have ventured to put them into print in his own time without being assured that the parties attacked could not reach him at law. We have an illustration of this in his references to Washington, Franklin, Schuyler, Colonels Meigs and Lamb, and others whose reputations he

seeks to bring under a cloud. Before taking up these names,
however, we may stop to inquire whether Judge Jones places
himself before history with quite the accuracy and candor expected of a writer with a judicial training. If he does not, we
are all the more prepared to discover that he fails in the same
respect in his treatment of others.

The Judge makes much of his own personal grievances.
The "Case of Thomas Jones, Esq." and its consideration both
from a public and private point of view, take up several pages
of the work. The author, as already stated, was seized or arrested at three different times during the course of the war—once
by the civil and twice by the military authorities. Respecting
the first arrest he appears to make no complaint, while the
other two he characterizes as dishonorable acts, reflecting in the
one case on Washington and in the other on Governor Trumbull, of Connecticut. But a brief review, even of his own facts,
may possibly compel a modification of this judgment.

In the eyes of the Revolutionary leaders in New York, the
Judge was an unqualified tory living on Long Island, and hence
a person not to be left at large to encourage toryism around
him. On the 19th of June, 1776, a Committee of the Provincial
Congress sent him notice to appear in New York on the 25th
of the same month and satisfy them whether he should be considered as "a friend to the American cause and of the number
of those who are ready to risque their lives and fortunes in defence of the rights and liberties of America." The Judge
doubtless having little inclination to recognize rebel authority
or avow before it his political sympathies, failed to put in an
appearance, and accordingly, two days later, on the 27th, was
arrested at his home and taken to New York upon the charge
of refusing to obey the Committee's summons. He was not
examined at this time, but on the 30th received a discharge
from Gouverneur Morris, the only member then in town, upon
giving the following parole :

"I certify that Thomas Jones, Esq., this day appeared before me a prisoner,
taken up by order of Congress, and having promised upon his word and honor
to appear at such time and place as a Committee of the Congress of this Colony
shall, upon reasonable notice to him given or left at his usual place of abode,
direct. The said Thomas Jones is therefore permitted to go unto, and reside at, his
usual place of abode, until the further order of the said Congress or Committee.
New York, June 30th, 1776.   GOUV. MORRIS."

Under this parole Judge Jones remained at his residence undisturbed until the 11th of August following. On that date he was arrested by order of General Washington and conducted to New York as one of the tories who could not safely be permitted to remain in the vicinity of the enemy. On the 12th he was brought before a Board of officers consisting of Lord Stirling, General Scott, General MacDougall, and Colonel Reed, and informed that he was "a prisoner to the American army" to be removed with others to the State of Connecticut, and "there to be disposed of in such manner as Governor Trumbull should think proper."

It is this second or military arrest that the Judge refers to as one of his particular grievances. He represents that when brought before the Board of officers they did not pretend that he was guilty of breaking the parole given to Gouverneur Morris, but justified his arrest on the ground of "prudence, necessity, and the custom of nations;" and out of this the Judge manufactures his charge. Speaking of himself in the third person he says (Vol. II. p. 276): "Mr. Jones lived upon Long Island, was a man of property, had great influence, and General Howe was expected to land upon the island every day, under which pretence *this flagrant breach of a solemn and sacred parole given by the civil power was justified by the rebel chief.*" In other words, the Judge evidently desires to be understood that Washington authorized his arrest irrespective of the Judge's obligations to the Provincial Congress—that the military deliberately nullified an engagement made between him and the civil authorities.

Viewed in any light this can hardly be regarded as other than a weak, if not a frivolous, charge for the Judge to prefer. It would possibly be a sufficient answer to say that war is war and the military supreme, that in extreme exigencies extreme measures are justified, and that if Washington deemed the Judge's arrest necessary from a military point of view his arrest should have been made regardless of his relations to any civil power. But what was this "solemn and sacred parole" which he gave to the Provincial Congress? Nothing more than a promise to answer its call whenever he should be summoned before it. It will be observed that it guarantees him no protection, nor does it prescribe his political conduct or restrain the exertion of his influence against the American cause as a condition of protection, nor does or could it promise him immunity from arrest by the military power. The parole was practically a notice to be ready "to appear;" it did not in the slightest degree limit or affect the future course or conduct of the American authorities, civil or military. They were each left free to treat the Judge and all other tories as the exigencies of the Campaign might require. The Judge was liable to be summoned by the Committee at any moment; he was equally liable to arrest by the military. Under these circumstances if the Congress finally turned the case over to the military authorities, can there be any question as to its right to do so? If both the civil and military powers were in perfect harmony in regard to the manner and propriety of the seizure, what could the Judge have to say in the matter? Could not the Congress waive all claim upon him if it so desired? Would it not have been obliged to waive its claim if the military saw fit to take up the case? and did not the Judge know, or ought he not to have known, that the civil power in that crisis was secondary, and that all considerations would have to yield to military "prudence" and "necessity"?

But referring to the facts again we find that the Judge and his fellow-tories were in reality treated with unusual consideration. They were arrested by Washington's order - the General being under no obligations whatever not to arrest them. When Washington was informed, however, that they did claim to be under a parole to answer the summons of the Congress (and he now seems to have heard of it for the first time), he proposed at once to relieve them of any fear they might have that the Congress would call for them when it would be out of their power to appear; and he immediately communicated the facts and his wishes to that body in a letter, dated August 12, as follows: "Some of these gentlemen have expressed doubts and raised difficulties, from engagements they lay under to your Honourable Body, or some Committees. They do not appear to me to deserve much attention, as they cannot with any propriety, be charged with a breach of any part under their present circumstances; but I beg leave to submit to your consideration the propriety of removing the pretence." The Congress in making their reply, *thanked the Commander-in-Chief for ordering the arrests,* and to settle all doubts in the matter of their paroles, passed the following resolution:

"*Whereas* certain members of the Convention, by authority from the same, did take the parol of sundry persons, inhabitants of this State; *And whereas* His Excellency Genl. Washington hath since found it necessary to cause some of the said persons to be made prisoners: Therefore,

"*Resolved unanimously,* That the said several parols be, and they hereby are, declared totally void, as to any obligations thereby laid upon those who have been, since the giving of the said parol, made prisoners as aforesaid." [1]

That Judge Jones and his fellow-prisoners well knew of this action appears from the Judge's own "Case," in which he states that he was informed that the parole was dissolved and that "an entry of its dissolution was made in the Journals of the Provincial Convention." When, therefore, the prisoners started for Connecticut and before their actual detention commenced they were bound by no paroles whatever, either civil or military.

Were anything further needed not only to justify but also to commend the course of the Commander-in-Chief in this matter it may be found in the general military situation already incidentally referred to. With the British at Staten Island threatening to move upon him at any hour, Washington properly assumed the exercise of every power required to thwart his antagonist and secure his own success. Among the measures regarded as imperative was the arrest of the principal tories and their removal from the scene of operations. It was a case of "military necessity," and on that ground fully justified. Washington's best vindication, in short, is his own letter on the subject addressed to the President of the Provincial Congress, the material part of which is as follows:

"HEAD QUARTERS, Aug. 12, 1776.

As the time is certainly near at hand and may be hourly expected, which is to decide the fate of this City, and the issue of this campaign, I thought it highly improper that persons of suspected character should remain in places where their opportunities of doing mischief were much greater than in the enemy's camp. I,

[1] *Journals Prov. Congress,* Vol. I. p. 570.

therefore, have caused a number of them to be apprehended and removed to some distance, there to remain until this crisis is passed. . . . . . I postponed this most disagreeable duty, till the last moment; but the claims of the army upon me, an application of a number of well-affected inhabitants, concurring with my own opinion, obliged me to enter upon it while time and circumstances would admit. I have ordered a very strict attention to be paid to the necessities of the gentlemen apprehended, and to their comfortable accommodation in every respect, both here and at the place of their destination." [1]

The proper representation of the case appears, then, to be this—that Washington was convinced, hostilities being imminent, that Judge Jones, as a dangerous tory, ought not to remain in the vicinity of New York; that he was justified in removing the Judge on the ground of military prudence and necessity; that any relations existing between the Judge and the civil authorities could not affect his duty as commander-in-chief of the army, even if he knew of the existence of such relations, which was evidently not the case; that upon his arrest he gave the Judge a hearing before a Board of officers; that when the Judge entered the plea that he was under obligations to the civil authorities, he was, by the civil authorities themselves, immediately released from those obligations; and that when he was finally sent off to Connecticut for confinement it was as a purely military prisoner resting under no parole whatsoever.

Under this state of facts how is it possible to entertain a charge of dishonorable conduct on the part of Washington? At what point in the case, it may be asked, does such conduct appear? All the facts, *per contra*, seem to unite to dissipate the charge, and it may be characterized as a lamentable failure—Washington's course throughout having been wise and politic, and his treatment of the Judge as honorable as it was considerate.

The next point concerns Governor Trumbull's experiences with the Judge. Arriving in Connecticut, "Mr. Jones" and his fellow-prisoners were there detained until the 9th of De-

[1] *Spark's Washington*, Vol. IV. p. 44.

cember following, when they were permitted to revisit their homes on signing a parole to give the enemy no assistance and return when called for. It was not until six months later that the Governor demanded their return. Not making their appearance, the demand was renewed, but again without effect. On each occasion the Governor transmitted his letters to the British headquarters by flags of truce, through the regular channels. Nothing further was done in the case until November, 1779, when it was proposed to attempt the capture of the Judge for the purpose of offering him in exchange for General G. Selleck Silliman, of the Connecticut State troops, who had lately been made prisoner by a party of tories from Long Island. The attempt succeeded, and Judge Jones once more found himself in the hands of the Connecticut authorities.

This final arrest or seizure—the third in his experience—is another of the Judge's personal grievances. He complains that he was surprised at his residence, forcibly taken therefrom, while still on his parole, and unjustly charged with violating his word of honor in not returning to Connecticut when called for. He declares emphatically (Vol. II. p. 292) that he was so charged by the Legislature of New York and the breach of his parole made a ground for attainting his person and property, and likewise so charged by Governor Trumbull, to whom he was immediately amenable, although, as the Judge continues to charge, both Legislature and Governor *knew* that he never received the notice of recall.

Deferring the action taken by New York for consideration in connection with the Act of Attainder, the Judge may be answered that, as for Governor Trumbull, his course, on the contrary, appears to have been entirely legitimate. He had the most substantial grounds for ordering the capture of the Judge on this last occasion, and there is no sufficient warrant for the insinuation that he charged the Judge with a personal breach of honor. Two or three original letters from the manuscript papers of the Connecticut Governor and of Governor Clinton, of New York, may here be introduced as throwing some light on the points in question. Thus after Judge Jones had been captured and brought to Fairfield, Connecticut, Governor Trumbull wrote to him as follows:

"(Copy.)   " LEBANON 12th November 1779

SIR It is now near two years since I wrote to you and the other gentlemen
from New York who were confined to this State, requesting their and your
return on your paroles—I have never yet received any satisfactory reason for a
non-compliance with that request. You will now be able to inform me your
reasons. I have given Mr. Deodate Silliman a Flag with letter to Sir Henry
Clinton, proposing your exchange for Gold Selleck Silliman, Esqr. A compliance
on the part of Sir Harry will obtain your permit on the present occasion to return
to New York. Notwithstanding this exchange, however, should it take place, I
shall still hold you answerable to your former parole given me when suffered
hertofore to go within the British Lines—

                                           I am Sir
                                           Your most obedient
                                                     hble servant,
THOMAS JONES Esqr, Prisoner at Fairfield." [1]   J—T—l.

In answer to this letter Judge Jones drew up an affidavit to
the effect apparently that he had never received any notification
from Governor Trumbull requiring his return, either through
the British Headquarters or any other channel, and that at
the time of his last arrest he was faithfully observing his original parole, given in December, 1776. This being satisfactory
to the Governor, the Judge was in time exchanged for General
Silliman. It appears also that with this exchange Governor
Trumbull wished to have nothing more to do with the Judge
and his fellow-tories, and transferred the care of them to Governor George Clinton of that State. In doing so he wrote
the following letter to Clinton explaining his action up to that
date :

                                          " LEBANON 10th March 1780
" SIR

      .   .   .   .

" You will also find enclosed five papers relative to Thos. Jones Esqr, who
was some time since taken from Long Island. Mr. Jones is one of those Gentlemen who were taken up in the State of N. York in the summer of 1776 and
sent on to this State for confinement as dangerous enemies to the American
cause.—And as it may be thought by those who are not acquainted with every
circumstance that Mr. Jones, (as having with the other Gentlemen referred to,
broken the conditions of the parole on which he and they were by me permitted
to return to the City of New York,) ought rather to be closely and rigorously
confined, than to be again liberated on parole or in Exchange—I have taken
particular care to enclose you an affidavit sworn to by Mr. Jones, as a previous
step to the Negotiation of Exchange of himself for Genl Silliman of the militia

[1] Trumbull Papers, vol. 20, p. 208. Mass. Hist. Society, Boston.

of this State.—And as this affidavit leads directly either to a suspicion of my
attention in this affair, or of the Honour of the British Commander in N. York, I
think it necessary to add that in the summer of 1777, 6 mo after these
gentn had been permitted to revisit their friends, a letter was written by me
to all of them collectively demanding their return agreeable to parole—which was
left with the officer commandg at the advanced post, beyond which the Flag was
not admitted.—That afterwards letters were written to each one separately of
similar import and delivered in the same manner—No answer has been received
to either of them.—In consequence of which my letter (a copy of which is en-
clos'd) to Sr Henry Clinton was forwarded—No answer has been received to
this, and it remains for you to determine on whom the imputation of Dishonor
shall rest—I beg leave to add that from this time I resign to you the further care
of these gentry to be dispos'd of as you shall see fit,—their paroles if you wish
them shall be sent on.

With all esteem and respect

I am Dr Sir

Your Most Obedient

& most Hble Servant,

Signed   J. TRUMBULL.

GOVR CLINTON N. York."[1]

To this letter Clinton replied briefly as follows:

"POUGHKEEPSIE May 1st 1780

SIR   I have been honored with your Excellency's Dispatch of the 10th
March last and its Enclosures some time since.

.   .   .   .   .   .

I am fully persuaded, Sir, that your Conduct towards Mr. Jones has been
strictly consistent and proper.   If the repeated notifications which you sent into
the british lines did not reach him it is his misfortune   Mr. Jones must be sensible that we cannot controul the enemy's officers within their lines—if they have
kept from him information regularly conveyed and in which he was so much interested it is to them he must apply for Redress.   Your Excellency will be
pleased to accept my thanks for the trouble you have taken in this Business and
I shall be obliged in having the Paroles of all the Gentry forwarded to me when
a convenient opportunity presents.

I have the honor to be,

with great Respect and Esteem,

Your Excellency's

Most Obedient Servant

GEO. CLINTON."[2]

[1] *Clinton Papers*, State Library, Albany.   First draft of it also in Mass.
Hist. Society's collections, *Letters and Papers* 1777-1780, p. 153.   The Judge's
affidavit referred to does not appear among the MS.

[2] *Clinton and Trumbull Papers*, Albany and Boston.   The omitted portion of
the letter refers to financial matters mentioned by Trumbull.

That these letters are of value in this connection will probably not be questioned. They indicate, first, that Governor Trumbull treated Judge Jones, after his capture, with all the fairness and consideration to which he was entitled. Certainly the Governor hints at no dishonorable conduct on the part of the Judge, as the latter alleges. His first step—an obviously proper and necessary requirement—was to request an explanation from the Judge for failing to appear when called for. That explanation proving valid and sufficient, the Judge was not held personally responsible for his non-appearance.

The letters, furthermore, furnish ample justification of the Governor's course in authorizing the seizure of the Judge on the occasion in question. The fact appears that Trumbull had three times demanded of the British authorities the return of the tory prisoners to Connecticut, and the demand had been ignored. They were not forthcoming. Either the prisoners themselves were guilty of a breach of faith, or the authorities were defying the Governor's power to enforce the observance of the paroles on which the prisoners had been permitted to return to their homes. Under these circumstances can there be any doubt as to the line of action which Trumbull would have been justified in pursuing thereafter? Can there be any doubt, for example, respecting his right to secure the return of the prisoners *by force*, if their re-arrest within the enemy's lines could be effected? Unquestionably he would have been justified in doing this, both to maintain his own authority and compel respect for the sanctity of paroles; and the seizure would have been justified entirely irrespective of the question whether Trumbull knew that the prisoners had or had not received the notification for their return to Connecticut. It was sufficient that they had been called for and had not come. It only remained, then, to seize them if possible. One of their number, Judge Jones, was seized and brought back to Connecticut. Can we question either the propriety, legality, or morality of the act? No doubt the Judge felt greatly abused, but as Governor Clinton suggests, it was from his own, the British authorities, that he should have sought satisfaction, and not from the American, who rightfully held him as their prisoner. It must thus appear, also, that when Judge Jones was seized, no necessary implication attached to that act that he had been *personally* guilty of a breach of faith. There is nothing in his own statement of the case or in the foregoing letters upon which it can be assumed that Trumbull believed he had broken his parole. On the contrary, if it be true, as the Judge represents, that the Governor *knew* that he had never received the notification to return, it is only proper to infer that the Governor could not have regarded him as personally chargeable with a breach of faith. That Trumbull would have declared the Judge responsible when he knew that he was not, is scarcely to be admitted.

The Judge's two charges against the Connecticut Governor are insufficiently supported. All the facts and circumstances tend to show that he was justified in seizing the Judge, and it nowhere appears that he charged him with a breach of his parole as a ground of his seizure.

If Judge Jones found himself by his last arrest in a trying and aggravating position, it was his own misfortune. If he voluntarily adhered to a side that esteemed him so lightly as not to notify him of his recall or protect him against recapture, he could make no complaint of any act of his enemies justified by the laws of war. It is difficult, in fact impossible, to discover wherein he was treated by those enemies, the Americans, in the matter of his arrests and paroles in any other than a fair and reasonable manner. His charge of dishonorable conduct on the part of Washington does not survive examination, and in regard to Trumbull's course, we have to concur with Governor Clinton that it was "strictly consistent and proper." The Judge's attempt to make himself a martyr at the expense of these two honored names is hardly creditable.

NOTE.

JUDGE JONES' EXCHANGE FOR GENERAL SILLIMAN.—Sir Henry Clinton and Governor Trumbull agreed to the exchange of the parties, soon after the Judge's capture; but before the exchange was completed, Clinton sailed on his

South Carolina expedition, leaving General Knyphausen in command at New York. Trumbull then wrote to Knyphausen in the matter and received reply Feb. 24, 1780, from Commissary Loring, that he was directed by General Knyphausen to state that General Clinton had left him no "instructions" for the exchange. (*Trumbull Papers*, Vol. XI. p. 71.) Trumbull accordingly wrote again, March 13, and enclosed to Knyphausen a copy of "the proposals made for the exchange of B. Genl. Silliman, &c., for T. Jones, Esq., &c., by Mr. Franklin and Majʳ Andre's consent. The Governor added: "I hope this measure will put an end to any further delay or objection to the execution of the proposed exchange, and have only to add that Mr. Jones shall be ordered in as soon as B. Genl Silliman shall be sent out to us." Trumbull also wrote to Governor William Franklin, President of the Board of Associated Loyalists, requesting him to furnish Knyphausen with the original proposals or Andre's consent. The Governor, furthermore, wrote on the same date to Judge Jones at Middletown, that he revoked the permission which had been given him to go into New York in exchange for General Silliman, until further orders, because, as he says, "those proposals being fully known in N. York give me some reason to suspect a Disposition at least to Delay if not to fully evade them." (*Trumbull Papers*, Vol. XX. pp. 236-238.) To Trumbull's letter of the 13th, Knyphausen replied on the 19th that he would "inquire particularly into the affair" and answer "in a short time." This answer does not appear on file among the Governor's papers, but it was doubtless favorable, and on the 27th of April following the exchange was finally effected.

The incidents of the exchange as given by Mrs. General Silliman (*Jones' History*, Vol. II., p. 565), may be supplemented by extracts from letters from the General himself, and his brother Deodate Silliman. The latter had charge of the Judge and sailed with him from Fairfield in the schooner Mifflin, of New London, at 9 A.M. April 27. "About three in the afternoon," he reports to the Governor, "I had the Pleasure of meeting the General off hart Island on his way to Fairfield to be exchangᵈ. We then Proceeded with Flaggs together to the Grand Duke guard ship off New City Island, where the master of the Flagg and myself ware taken on board, and the exchange was then compleated By my giving a Receipt that I had Recᵈ the General, and taking Receipt that I had Delivered Mr. Jones in Exchange for him—which I beg leave to Transmitt to your Excellency."

General Silliman's letter, written to the Governor (*Papers*, Vol. XI p. 1070), is as follows

"FAIRFIELD, May 2d 1780

Sir Last Fryday evening, I had the satisfaction again to return from captivity to my Family and Friends, and once more to breathe the Air of Liberty and Freedom.

I left New York on Wensday last on Parole, in order to come Home to procure your Excellency's Permission for Mr. Jones to be sent in in Exchange for me. On Thursday about Three of the Clock in the afternoon, I happily met Mr. Jones in the Sound near Hart Island, going in under your Excellency's Flag in order that I might come out exchanged. We immediately put back, and came under the Stern of the Guard Ship the *Grand Duke*, commanded by Capt. Holman, which lay between New City Island and Hart Island. The Exchange was there made, and we having exchanged vessels, Mr. Jones proceeded immediately for New York, having the wind and tide for him, but I was detained by the same means that carried him on till the next morning, and then made sail and got Home at evening.

And now Hon'. Sir give me Leave to return your Excellency my most sincere Thanks for the many Favours that I have in Time past experienced from your Excellency, and Especially for your late particular attention to every measure that tended to return me to the Blessings of Liberty and Freedom.

The Deputy Commissary of Prisoners when I parted with him threatened that they would soon have me again. . . .

I am Your Excellency's
Most Obedient
Humble Servant
G. SELLECK SILLIMAN.

His Excellency Gov'. TRUMBULL."

III.—THE CASE OF COLONEL MEIGS.

Passing from Judge Jones' "Case," that of Colonel Meigs may next be taken up as an illustration of the author's method in his treatment of others. So far as his estimates of character appear to be mere impressions formed by the Judge in a disturbed and prejudiced state of mind, they will be accepted for what they are worth; but where he enters into facts as the basis of his opinion, a proper regard for the reputation of men who in their day rendered good service, requires a verification of the facts themselves. In the case of Meigs we have a remarkable piece of judicial or historical portraiture, whichever it may be.

Colonel Return Jonathan Meigs, of the Connecticut line, stands among the famous officers of his rank in the Revolutionary army. His name is identified with Arnold's expedition against Quebec, a brilliant exploit at Sag Harbor, Long Island, the storming of Stony Point, and the various movements along the Hudson until 1781. He closed an honorable life in 1823 as

the government's agent among the Cherokee Indians, by whom
he was affectionately called the "White Path" in appreciation
of his integrity and friendship. Against this officer, whose character has ever been above reproach, Judge Jones now brings
three charges, namely, (1.) that he was a pardoned felon, (2.)
that he deliberately broke his parole, and (3.) that he headed the
"conspiracy" of the American prisoners at Quebec in 1776. A
fourth charge connected with the case is to the effect that the
Continental Congress *knew* that Meigs was a violator of the public faith and yet approved his conduct and rewarded his services.
What the Judge says of the Colonel, after giving an account of
his Sag Harbor expedition in the spring of 1777, is as follows
(vol. 1, p. 181), the italics being, in this and other quotations,
the present writer's:

"This Meigs was a native of Connecticut, of a reputable family, and large
connections. A few years before the war, he had been detected in New York in
passing counterfeit paper money in imitation of the lawful paper money of that
colony, knowing the same to be counterfeit. This crime, by the laws of New
York, was felony without the benefit of clergy. For this he was apprehended,
imprisoned, indicted, tried, convicted, sentenced to be hanged, and a day fixed for
the execution. But upon a joint application of the Governor, the Council and
General Assembly of Connecticut, to the Governor of New York in behalf of the
prisoner, he was by the latter, with the advice of his Majesty's Council, pardoned
and discharged. When the disturbances began in America he obtained a commission in the Connecticut troops and was with the army before Boston in 1775.
When Arnold undertook to march from thence by the way of the Kennebeck
across the country, and assist Montgomery in the siege of Quebec, Meigs turned
out as a volunteer, and upon this occasion obtained a majority. When Montgomery attempted to storm the garrison, Meigs was of the party. Upon the fall
of Montgomery and the defeat of his party, Meigs was among a number of other
rebels taken prisoners. The prisoners were detained in Quebec during the winter
and civilly treated. They had rations equally with the King's troops. Such of the
privates as were in want of clothes were by the humanity of General Carleton sup-
plied with every necessity. The officers had the liberty of the town upon parole.
The common men were confined in comfortable commodious places. The officers
had the liberty of visiting the men whenever they pleased. While thus enjoying
all the comforts that prisoners could wish or desire, they entered into a conspiracy,
(*of which Meigs was at the head*) to seize the garrison. The night and hour was
fixed upon, and the rebels forming the blockade had notice of it. They were to
attack the town without, and while the garrison should, upon the alarm, repair to
their several places of duty, Meigs and the other prisoners were to make an attack within. Of this conspiracy the Government got timely notice. The officers
were of course taken up, and with the men, closely confined during the winter. In
July, 1776, General Carleton sent the whole of them by water to the several prov-

inces to which they respectively belonged, first taking their paroles not to take up arms against Great Britain until exchanged. *Under this parole was Meigs when he performed his Sag Harbor expedition.* This Congress knew, yet, so far from disapproving of such a breach of honour, of faith, and veracity, they not only voted him the thanks of their body, which were transmitted in a letter signed by their President, but presented him with a silver-hilted sword of considerable value. Whether General Howe ever complained to Congress of this flagrant violation of public faith I know not. But this I know, if he did, he got no satisfaction. Congress *approved the act* and rewarded the man."

These are serious accusations, and if true, let in a ray of unpleasant light upon some of the methods adopted by our ancestors to secure the success of the Revolution. But they *all fail* when compared with records more authoritative than Judge Jones' manuscript. Were no other records existing, the inherent improbability of the charges ought to be their own refutation. Can it be assumed, for example, that a despicable character, such as Meigs is pictured, should have been permitted to hold an officers' commission in the King's Colonial militia service prior to the Revolution, that thereafter Trumbull and Washington should have appointed him a Colonel in the Continental army, and that subsequently the Government should have retained him for many years to the close of his life in a public position of honor and trust? The imputations are unworthy of credit, and the documents in the case dispose of them finally. Thus two of the charges, making Colonel Meigs a parole breaker and declaring Congress to have been cognizant of the fact, are disproved by the following note from Washington's Headquarters, written by Colonel Webb, of the Commander-in-Chief's staff, and published in the *Connecticut Gazette* of New London, January 31, 1777 :

" HEAD QUARTER IN MORRISTOWN, Jan. 10, 1776 [1777].

I have it in command from his Excellency General Washington, to request you will publish the following list of gentlemen, officers and volunteers, *who are released from their parole*, which they gave General Carleton, by an exchange of others of the same rank and number belonging to the British army.

I am &c.,

Samuel B. Webb, A.D.C.

Majors *Meigs*, Bigelow, Captains, *Lamb*, Tobham, Thayer, Morgan, Goodrich, Hanchett ; Lieutenants McDougall, Compton, Clark, Webb, Feger [Febiger], Heth, Savage, Brown, Nicholls, Bruin, Steel ; Ensign, Tisdal ; Volunteers, Oswald, Duncan, Lockwood, McGuire, Potterfield, Henry "

As the Sag Harbor expedition was not undertaken until
May 23d following, we find from Colonel Webb's letter that
Meigs was *regularly exchanged four months and more* before the
time when Judge Jones claims that he was still under his
parole.[1] The Colonel's honor is thus clearly vindicated ; so also
is that of Congress, whose members are charged with being
fully informed of an act which was never committed. The
Judge's tirade against that body, quoted above, is founded on
nothing and comes to nothing.

The second and more odious charge representing Colonel
Meigs as a criminal before the war must be characterized as a
gross libel upon the memory of a worthy man and brave soldier,
the individual described by the Judge as a pardoned counter-
feiter being quite another character, one *Felix* Meigs and not
Return Jonathan, nor belonging to the same family. Abundant
proof of this existing in manuscript could be spread out were it
necessary, or did the documents furnish anything of historical
interest. It is enough to know that the Judge blundered un-
pardonably when he identified the Colonel as the culprit—un-
pardonably because he failed to assure himself that he had not
blundered. Nor does the Judge state the case precisely, although his opportunities for accuracy were good, he being a
judicial officer at the time in New York and his father one of
the judges of the court which tried Felix. This person, who
was engaged in the boating trade around the city, was brought
up before the July term of the Court in the year 1772. Before
sentence was carried out, however, a few of his friends in Connecticut petitioned Governor Trumbull to request Governor
Tryon, of New York, to pardon him upon the ground of his
previous good character and certain extenuating circumstances
in the case ; and upon this ground Trumbull laid the matter before Tryon. The Legislature of Connecticut had nothing to do

---

[1] The date of Colonel Meigs' exchange is of some consequence. If he was not
exchanged until March, 1777, as stated in the Note on this subject in Vol. I. p.
668, he was then violating his parole, for he had been promoted to be Lieut.-
Colonel from a Majority, and was on active duty. The authority given for March
is Judge Henry ; but the Judge makes no mention of the exchange. The true
date is January 1st. See Biographical Sketch of Col. Meigs in *Mag. of American
History* for April, 1880.

with it. Governor Tryon, who at that time maintained the friendliest relations with his Connecticut neighbor, referred the case to his council on the 8th of September following, and was advised by them to postpone action until his " Majesty's Pleasure" could be ascertained. This was communicated in due time by Lord Dartmouth, in a letter dated " Whitehall Dec' 9", 1772" leaving the final determination in Tryon's hands, who thereupon signed a full pardon for Felix under date of April 19, 1773.[1]

This brief statement will doubtless be accepted as sufficient to identify the person whom Judge Jones had in mind when he penned the libel on the distinguished Continental Colonel. As he appears to have remembered so many particulars of the case, the query suggests itself how he happened to fail in the important particular of names and brand the wrong man with infamy.

The remaining charge or assertion that Colonel Meigs headed the Quebec Conspiracy has no force, since that conspiracy was nothing more than a justifiable attempt on the part of the prisoners to make their escape ; but as the Judge evidently regards it as a serious offence, it may be asked whether the enemy would have so far favored this " ringleader" as to permit him to return home on parole before any of his companions, and that, too, but a few weeks after the detection of his plot ? Nor was the consideration he received on leaving Quebec quite such as would be accorded a desperate conspirator—Captain Dearborn, who alone returned with Meigs, giving us in his manuscript journal a brief account of their departure as follows :

" May 16. [1776] .   . At 5 : of the clock the Town Major came for Major Meigs & myself, to go to the Lieut. Governor to give our Parole—the verbal agreement we made was that if ever there was an exchange of Prisoners, we were to have the benefit of it and until then we were not to take up arms against the King.—After giving our Parole from under our hands, we were carried before the Genl., who appear'd to be a very humane tender-hearted man. After wishing us a good voyage, & saying he hoped to give the remainder of our officers the same Liberty, he desir'd the Town Major to conduct us on Board—we desired leave to visit our men in prison but could not obtain it—after getting our baggage & taking leave of our fellow prisoners we went on board a schooner, which we

[1] *New York Colonial Manuscripts*, vol. 99, p. iii, and vol. 100, p. 48. Secretary of State's office, Albany, N. Y.

are to go to Halifax in, but as she did not sail to-day, · *are invited on Board the Admiral's ship, where we were very genteely used, and Tarried all night."[1]

There is but one comment to be made on this case : Every material damaging statement regarding Colonel Meigs—four in number, if the last can be included—is found to be *false throughout.*

IV.—THE CASE OF COLONEL LAMB.

The next case is that of Colonel John Lamb, of New York City, commanding the Fourth Continental Artillery Regiment, whom Judge Jones couples with Meigs as another flagrant parole-breaker among Washington's officers. The passage containing the charge is as follows, the author referring to Lamb with seemingly derisive familiarity as "John" (Vol. II. p. 342):

"When the Stamp Act was passed by the British Parliament, John took an active part in opposition to it, was a mighty leader, and haranguer, among the 'Mobility.' The Act being repealed and peace restored, John's popularity ceased. There was nothing left to keep it up. When the late troubles commenced John again rose into consequence ; he headed mobs, excited sedition, talked treason, abused the Loyalists, harangued the populace, and damned the Tories. Upon General Lee's dismantling Fort George, and the Batteries in New York, of their cannon and stores, in the spring of 1775, and removing them into the Fields, John was made Master-General of the ordnance. And dressed in blue and buff, he afterwards joined Montgomery in Canada, was wounded, and taken prisoner, at Quebec. A number of others were also taken at the same place. General Carleton sent all the prisoners to their respective Colonies, taking their paroles not to bear arms against Great Britain, until regularly exchanged. John was a restless spirit, could not bear to be idle, and had little honour. In April, 1777, he was in the attack upon Danbury, and was, *notwithstanding his parole,* defending Fort Constitution when taken by General Clinton in October, 1777. He luckily made his escape."

Here again is an accusation which cannot stand, Colonel Lamb having *faithfully observed his parole* until properly exchanged in January, 1777, three months before his participation in any military enterprise. Colonel Webb's letter naming Lamb with Meigs in the list of exchanged prisoners is sufficient proof in the case, but to it may be added the official papers

---

[1] *Dearborn's MS. Journal* in possession of the Boston Public Library.

printed in Leake's Life of Lamb. One of these is a memorial to Congress, dated November 25, 1776, in which we have this officer's own sense of the obligation he was under. An extract from it is as follows:

" *To the Honorable Congress of the United States of America.*

GENTLEMEN Altho' the Enemy have, contrary to my expectations, liberated me from the dreary Horrours of a Prison, and suffered me to return to my family and friends, I am still subject to their power and controul ; liable to be called upon by them to surrender myself a prisoner whenever they please ; and restrained by the sacred ties of honour from drawing my sword again in defence of my country till exchanged for some officer of theirs. Extremely anxious to be relieved from this truly painful and disagreeable situation, I waited on General Washington immediately after my arrival from Quebec, earnestly soliciting his interest with your Honours for that purpose. But as I have not yet heard that such an event had taken place—owing, I imagine, to the critical situation of the two armies ; I take the liberty to address your Honours on that subject, humbly requesting that I may be included in the next exchange of Prisoners."

Four days later Congress received this petition, and immediately *resolved :* " That the General be directed to include Major Lamb in the next exchange of Prisoners;" and that an exchange was speedily effected, and the Major released appears from the following notification from Colonel Knox at Washington's headquarters :

" TRENTON, Jan'y 2, 1776 [1777]
SIR I have the pleasure to acquaint you, that Gen. Howe *has consented to your exchange, and sent out the parole which you gave Gen. Carleton.* His Excellency, Gen. Washington wishes to provide for you in proportion to your great merits, and wishes to see you as soon as possible.
I am Sir with
esteem, your most
ob & hble Servt.
H. KNOX
Commanding the Artillery
Major LAMB of the United States."

While these documents definitely settle the parole question in favor of Colonel Lamb and against Judge Jones, it may be observed as in the case of Colonel Meigs, that even were this evidence wanting it cannot be supposed that Lamb would have been permitted to hold an active military command, especially at so important a post as Fort Montgomery, when at any moment he could be demanded by and returned to the enemy as one of their prisoners. John Lamb, we suspect, was too stirring a Son of Liberty and too unctious a hater of tories to escape uncomplimentary and vindictive mention by the Judge; but what the Judge writes about him with apparently the best relish turns out again to be a libel.[1]

—— — ·

V.—THE JUDGE'S CHARGES AGAINST WASHINGTON. WASHINGTON'S PAROLE.

The third military personage whom the "learned" Judge attempts to drag into disgrace is none other than the American Commander-in-Chief; for we are given to understand that he not only broke his parole in his younger days, but that during the Revolution, his conduct more than once was marred with coarseness, severity, and actual cruelty. The charge of parole-breaking might have been anticipated. A writer who could readily believe that Washington suffered Colonels Meigs and Lamb to assume their regular duties in the army before being exchanged would have little hesitation in questioning the honor of the Chief himself in the matter of observing his own parole. But, inevitably, the Judge again comes to grief with his charge, as appears from the editor's own notes on this point. The charge (Vol. II. p. 346) is to the effect that when taken prisoner at Little Meadows in 1754, in the French and Indian War, Washington "pledged his honour not to bear arms against France for twelve months," but that nevertheless he was found fighting "under the banners of Braddock, upon the Monongahela" before the year was up. This accusation, however, meets two obstinate facts. *First.* All that the French demanded of Washington and his party was a promise *not to work upon any buildings or forts west of the mountains* during the year beginning with the date of the capitulation. Otherwise they were left free to serve as English soldiers.

---

[1] The documents from the Life of Lamb, quoted above, appear not to be entirely satisfactory to the editor of Jones' work, who states that the Judge was *probably* mistaken about Lamb's parole, and that he simply recorded what was generally believed at the time. General Knox's letter ought to be conclusive. It would be interesting also to know what evidence exists showing that there was a belief current that Lamb had broken his parole; and did it become a Judge to publish a libel on mere rumor?

Washington's presence with Braddock, therefore, was not a violation of his parole. *Second.* An interval of *more than twelve months* elapsed between the Little Meadows surrender and Braddock's disaster; so that in any case there would have been no breaking of the pledge given to the French. The Judge took up report or supposition and attempted to make history out of it.

WASHINGTON AND TORY RAIL-RIDING.

Not content with preferring this charge against Washington— a charge which, if proven, would alone be sufficient to lower him in the estimation of posterity—the Judge proceeds to hold him up in another light. He lays stress in particular upon the conduct of the Chief in the case of the British Captain Asgill, which attracted much attention towards the close of the war, and also upon the satisfaction with which he is alleged to have looked upon the persecution of New York tories on a certain occasion in 1776. As to the latter case, it appears that on the 12th of June a number of the Sons of Liberty and others ferreted out several specially obnoxious tories, and rode them on rails through the city. According to the Judge they were carried from point to point and their offences duly proclaimed. Occasionally the mob would stop, indulge in some jeering demonstration, and then move on (Vol. I, p. 102).

"The like proclamations," continues the Judge, "were made before the City Hall, where the provincial Convention was then sitting forming laws for the civil government of the province; before exchange where the committee were sitting making rules and regulations for preserving the good order, the peace and quiet of the city; and before the door of General Washington, who pretended the army under his command was raised for the defence of *American Liberty,* for the preservation of the *rights of mankind,* and for the protection of America against the unjust usurpations of the British ministry. Notwithstanding which, so far did this humane General, and the two public bodies aforesaid, approve of this unjustifiable mob, that it received the sanction of them all. They appeared at the windows, raised their hats, returned the huzzas and joined in the acclamations of the multitude. Nay so far did General Washington give his sanction of, and approbation to, this inhuman barbarous proceeding that he gave a very severe reprimand to General Putnam, who accidentally meeting one of the processions in the street, and shocked with its barbarity, attempted to put a stop to it, Washington declaring that to discourage such proceedings was to injure the cause of liberty in which they were then engaged, and that nobody would attempt it but an enemy to his country."

The reader will doubtless agree with the Judge that rail-riding
is an "unmerciful" and unnecessary proceeding in any case;
but it cannot be assumed that many will agree with him that the
story he tells here respecting Washington's approval of the mob
is grounded in truth. Washington is to be found uniformly on
the side of order and humanity. His treatment of tories, even
when they showed themselves "the most inveterate enemies,"
was neither severe nor unprecedented. We have his views on
this point expressed but a short time after the occurrence noted
above, when Governor Livingston sought his advice on the propriety of permitting certain disaffected persons to return to their
homes. Washington replied that such permission could be given
to those whom the Governor knew and could trust, but adds:
"I would suggest to you, that my tenderness has been often
abused, and I have had reason to repent the indulgence shown
them; *I would show them all possible humanity and kindness, consistent with our own safety;* but matters are now too far advanced to sacrifice anything to punctilios." This is not the lan-
guage of a General who delighted in rail-riding processions.

But as a matter of fact the military did disperse the mob,
and the evidence is strong that it was done by express command
of Washington himself. Ensign Caleb Clap, an eye-witness,
refers to the affair as follows:[1]

"June 11" [12'']—the Citizens of the City of New York Gethered together a
number of them and went round among them which they supposed to be tories,
striped a number of them and was at the Trouble of carrying them about the
Streets on a Raii, and then confined them in Geol—others they Visited and they
appeared to be so Humble they Let them alone after making Promise to comply
with their Directions (I happened to have the Command of the Picquet that Day)
the General Sent for all the Picquets in the three Brigades in order to Surpress
them but seeing so many under Arms they Dispersed Quick."

It seems to be entirely legitimate to infer that the "General"
mentioned here as sending for the pickets was the Commander-
in-Chief. The Ensign elsewhere refers to him in the same way,
and does not use the word to indicate any other General. In
addition, the "three Brigades" mentioned included the entire

[1] *Diary of Ensign Caleb Clap*, Col. Baldwin's Mass. Regt., in Hist. Mag.,
Third Series, March, 1874, p. 135.

army at New York at that date, and received orders direct from
Washington. And as to the statement that Gen. Putnam was
severely reprimanded by his Chief, for interfering with the march
of the mob, it sinks under its own inconsistency. Putnam was
not the only general officer who appeared on the scene. The
Moravian pastor Shewkirk states that " *Some of the generals,
and especially Putnam and their forces, had enough to do to
quell the riot, and make the mob disperse;*" [1] and it is on official
record that after order was restored, Putnam *accompanied by
General Mifflin,* who at that time had Washington's confidence
as much as any officer in the army, proceeded to the New York
Convention and complained of the day's doings on the part of
the citizens.[2] That body immediately passed resolutions disapproving the mob. If Washington dealt out reprimands im-
partially on the occasion, he must have had some for Mifflin and
other officers, and a certain amount for the Convention. Judge
Jones' version of the incident sounds like a piece of sensational
reporting. There is no indication that he was present and saw
what he describes—the very account itself, indeed, being evidence of his absence. He has clearly given us hearsay or imagination again; certainly, it is not history.

VI.—FRANKLIN AND HIS SON, THE NEW JERSEY GOVERNOR.

The Judge's reference to Benjamin Franklin (Vol. I. p. 135)
is another pretended revelation of discreditable secret history.
The statement is to the effect that when Connecticut, according to
the Judge, became alarmed at the military outlook in December,
1776 (still another absurdity to be exposed), her authorities
released all the prisoners in their power with a single exception.
This exception was the royal Governor William Franklin, of
New Jersey, who, we are informed, was not only " detained and
most inhumanly treated," but that "*at the request of his
father, the arch rebel, Dr. Franklin.*" But if the records are to
be trusted this assertion is as unfounded in fact as it is heartless.
    Governor Franklin was detained in Connecticut solely in

consequence of his own insidious hostility to the Revolution, and if his confinement at a later date was close and rigid, his own conduct gave the occasion. Upon his arrest in June, 1776, as the obstructive governor of New Jersey, he was transferred to Connecticut for safe keeping, where he was quartered first at Wallingford and then at Middletown upon a liberal parole. On the 23d of November following, Congress proposed that Franklin be exchanged for General William Thompson, of Pennsylvania, who was a prisoner in Canada. But ten days later, December 3d, that body reversed its action by resolving to suspend the exchange until further orders, upon the ground, as stated by Hancock, that the liberation of Franklin at that critical period might prove "prejudicial and attended with some bad consequences" to the American cause.[1] Now when these resolves were passed by Congress, Benjamin Franklin, the father, *was on the Atlantic*, making his voyage to France as one of the American Commissioners to the Court of Versailles, and was as ignorant of the above proceedings regarding his son, the Governor, as Judge Jones, "the acute eye-witness," appears to have been. The simple fact is that Congress would have exchanged Franklin had not our reverses in New Jersey, where Franklin's influence would have been considerable, rendered the exchange unadvisable. It was the turn in the military situation and not his father's "request" that led to the Governor's detention in Connecticut.

The further libellous insinuation that it was Dr. Franklin's desire that his son should be "inhumanly treated" stands probably on the same intangible authority with the previous charge. In April, 1777, when "undoubted information" reached Congress that Governor Franklin, while on parole at Middletown, had sedulously employed himself in scattering Howe's proclamations of pardon about him, thus aiding the enemies of the United States, that body directed Governor Trumbull to have him closely confined without the use of pen, ink, or paper, or the access of any persons without the Governor's permission. Franklin was then removed to Litchfield, Connecticut, and carefully guarded. In July, 1777, he applied for a release on parole

[1] *Force*, 5th Series, Vol. III. p. 1069.

to visit his sick wife in New Jersey, but Congress charged that
he had again abused his parole, accusing him of the violation of
"so sacred a tie as that of honor," and declined, despite his
urgent plea, to allow him any freedom within the American
lines. This treatment he characterized as cruel in the extreme,
while Congress justified its course on the ground of the public
safety and loss of confidence in his word.

The Governor was finally exchanged in the fall of 1778, as a
prisoner of war, and sent into New York. All this time his
father was in France, practically beyond the reach of Congress,
which obviously in this matter decided for itself upon every new
phase of the Governor's case. Father and son reconciled their
personal and political alienation at the close of the war, but we
hear nothing of this "inhuman treatment" among the recollections to be forgotten.

VII.—CONNECTICUT IN DECEMBER, 1776.

Leaving the reputations of Washington, Franklin, Meigs,
and Lamb unblemished, so far as Judge Jones's attempt to
defame them is concerned, we may look into certain other statements of this contemporary historian. There are several sufficiently suspicious, upon their face, to court investigation, one of
which seriously affects what Colonel Harry Lee calls in his
"Memoirs" "the faithful State of Connecticut." If the Judge
is correct, Lee complimented that State far beyond her deserts,
as must appear from the following, in Vol. I. pp. 134 5 :

"So far did Connecticut look upon the contest with Great Britain as over
that in December, 1776, the Great and General Court not only released every
prisoner in their power (except Governor Franklin, who was detained and most
inhumanly treated, and that at the request of his father, the arch rebel, Dr.
Franklin), but actually appointed and empowered a committee of their body to
proceed to New York, to make submission to the King's Commissioners, to ask a
restoration to the King's peace; and, if possible, to preserve their charter from
forfeiture, their estates from confiscation, and their persons from attainder. But
the unfortunate action at Trenton, which happened shortly after, and the conse-
quent transactions in New Jersey, put an end to this favorable disposition in the
inhabitants of Connecticut."

This surprising statement, if true, places Connecticut, his-
torically, in a craven position compared with that of her sister-

States at that time. No other showed the least disposition, through its Legislature, to commit such base tergiversation, which must be regarded as all the baser in the case of Connecticut, when we recall the enthusiasm with which her train-bands marched to Boston upon the Lexington alarm, and the large number of troops she furnished the army in 1776. All her previous political professions, moreover, had been upon the side of resistance.

The accuracy of the foregoing quotation is assumed in the " Notes" (Vol. 1. p. 641) upon the ground that the Judge was a prisoner in Connecticut at that date, with opportunities for information, and hence "not likely to be mistaken." But judging from the experience and fate of other statements on his part, the Judge's opportunities for observation fail to make him any more of an authority, and it will not be an exceptional incident if we find the records in the present case once more offering a complete contradiction to his assertions.

Connecticut not only did not look upon the contest as over in December, 1776, but on the contrary *increased her exertions at home, encouraged her soldiers in camp, and prepared in the most energetic manner for the continuation of the struggle.* To enter into any extended proof of this must appear superfluous. The record is clear and certain. It was on the very darkest of the dark days of 1776—December 28—that Governor Trumbull wrote to Washington : " The disposition and spirit of the inhabitants of this State is *unaltered,* but we are weakened by the constant demand of men and every kind of clothing." On December 7, the same day that the Governor's council permitted Judge Jones and his fellow-prisoners to return to their homes on parole, he wrote :

" The General Assembly of this State, *sensible of the vast importance of upon the great cause in which you are so nobly struggling,* have, at their session of the 10th of November last, made provision for raising by enlistment four battalions to serve under your command until the 5th of March next, before which time I have strong hopes our quota of the Continental army will be completed; and I do earnestly recommend it to the brave officers and soldiers of this State now in your army freely and cheerfully to undertake in defence of so great, so just, and so good a cause. The misery and wretchedness to which they and their families, their friends, and their country must be reduced if our enemies succeed are dreadful in idea; how much more dreadful and how intolerable to be realized!"

Many other similar expressions could be quoted, and it is to be observed that they are expressions of fidelity to the cause made by a Governor officially representing a like fidelity on the part of its Legislature.

Furthermore, the November and December sessions of the Connecticut Assembly, which, according to the Judge, debased itself so far as to offer submission to the enemy, were special sessions *held for war purposes.* The last resolution adopted at the November sitting declared expressly that "the situation of the army, the great necessity of providing and forwarding, the raising of the new army, and of putting the militia upon the best footing, and the probability of soon receiving further intelligence from Congress and the army, very interesting to this and the other States, would speedily require a further session." Upon this the Assembly met again on the third Wednesday in December at Middletown. These two sessions were held during the most critical period of the campaign, but all their acts and resolutions, of which an official summary is preserved in the Connecticut archives, were of a highly public-spirited and determined character. All private bills were postponed and the needs of the hour alone attended to. It was voted to thoroughly reorganize the militia, to recruit new regiments for State and Continental service, to offer liberal bounties, to establish a loan-office to raise money to purchase arms, manufacture cannon, and prepare generally for a vigorous defence. Those troops whose term of service was to expire in December were urged by the Assembly to remain longer with Washington, should he need them, "*for the sake of their country and all its inestimable rights, themselves, and all posterity.*" To check the exorbitant charges for provisions made by monopolizers, or that "class of men who preferred their own private gain *to the interest, comfort, and safety of the country,*" an act was passed governing the price of labor and the necessaries of life. Commissaries in the different parts of the State were directed to give information against all persons "purchasing up and engrossing" articles of clothing needed for the soldiers. Word coming that the troops in the Continental service were suffering from the want of blankets, the selectmen of all the towns were charged with procuring blankets at once, and "if a sufficient number could not be obtained in

this manner, that a warrant should issue to supply the deficiency
by impressment." Cannon were sent to Norwalk and Green-
wich for their defence, and the Governor and Council authorized
to supply the towns with "such quantity of powder" as they
might require ; and much more to the like effect. But perhaps
the most significant action on the part of the Assembly was
that taken in December, when news came that the enemy were
making their way through New Jersey towards Philadelphia,
and that the inhabitants of Pennsylvania were hurrying to
Washington's assistance. It was then resolved to encourage the
patriotism " so boldly manifested," and to call upon " any and
all able-bodied men in Connecticut, residing west of Connecticut
River, cheerfully to go forward and offer themselves for the service of their country on so great an occasion." A Committee
also was appointed to repair to that part of the State " *to arouse
and animate the people to rise and exert themselves, with the
greatest expedition, to cherish and propagate the spirit, zeal, and
ardor for the country, to set on foot with all expedition an enlistment in the various parts of the State; and all friends of the country
were earnestly exhorted to lend all their aid to said Committee, to
promote so great and good a design.*" So, too, when Sir Henry
Clinton landed in Rhode Island and threatened an invasion of
the New England States, and it was proposed that a Committee
from those States should meet at Providence on the 23d of
December to provide " for their mutual and immediate defence
and safety," the Connecticut Assembly appointed Messrs. Titus
Hosmer, Eliphalet Dyer, Richard Law, and Nathaniel Wales,
Jr., leading men in the State, " a Committee to meet the Committees of New England, at Providence, or at any other place at
the time aforesaid, or as soon as might be, *to consult of the expedi-
ency of raising and appointing an army for the more immediate
defence of New England, against the threatened invasions, as well
as for a more general defence in the common cause.*"

Little confirmation does this record—and there is much more
of the same sort—contribute in support of Judge Jones's assertion
that Connecticut, in December, 1776, or at any other time,
looked upon the contest as over, and fell upon her knees to
beg for peace. It follows, necessarily, that the two proofs he
advances to sustain his general charge, namely, that a Committee

was appointed to make submission to the King's Commissioners and that all the prisoners in the State were released, have nothing to stand upon. The resolutions and utterances of the Assembly, above referred to, are a flat denial of the first. Could that body have had the simplicity to imagine that the King's Commissioners would receive their Committee with open arms, and engage "to preserve their charter from forfeiture, their estates from confiscation, and their persons from attainder," when their public proceedings at the very time were nothing less than successive acts of rebellion and resistance? Or could that Committee have guaranteed, on condition of pardon, to restore the State to its former allegiance, when its best people were already in arms or arming either for the militia or Continental service? Or could such a Committee have been appointed without opposition, and that opposition not showing itself outside of the Assembly and exciting public discussion? If Judge Jones knew of the appointment of such a Committee, how is it that no one else heard of it—General Howe, for instance, or Governor Tryon, who were quick to report to the home government any sign of a favorable disposition on the part of the colonists? The Judge's assertion is obviously absurd if not malicious. The Connecticut Assembly could have appointed no Committee for the purpose represented.

In the Judge's second point—the alleged release of prisoners through *fear*—we have simply a second perversion of fact. The tory prisoners—"disaffected" persons—of whom Judge Jones was one, had been sent from New York into Connecticut at different dates during the year, some of them having been separated from their families several months. It appears that in December, a number of these were released, but not as the Judge implies, in the sense of being set free because the State was ready to give up the contest. They were simply *permitted*, and that upon *their own application*, to return to their homes and neglected private affairs upon parole to say and do nothing prejudicial to the American cause and to report back to Connecticut when demanded. The Judge, in fact, contradicts himself on this point; for while in the extract quoted above, he alleges that the prisoners (himself included) were released in consequence of Connecticut's fright, he elsewhere twice asserts,

once under oath (Vol. II. pp. 276, 299), that Governor Trumbull
gave him *permission* to return home and the Governor in the
manuscript letter to Governor Clinton uses the same word in
the same connection clearly in the sense that the act was an
official *favor*. Such it was well understood to be by the other
prisoners. Thus Benjamin Whitehead, Richard Betts, and
George Hewlett, prominent tories of New York, sign paroles on
December 21, 1776, which contain the following clause :   . . .
" Whereas, *upon our application*, his Honor Jonathan Trumbull,
Esq., Governor of said State of Connecticut, *hath permitted us
to return to our families in New York*," etc.   Thus Colonel Fred-
erick Phillips, Hugh Wallace, James Jauncey, James Jauncey, Jr.,
Gerard Walton, William Jauncey, John Miller, and others of the
same place all *apply* for paroles. Thus Samuel Burling and
Robert A. Waddell, who were denied permission in consequence
of improper conduct at their quarters a short time before, put
in a plea of intoxication and say : " We hope your Honour,
and the Honorable Council, will reconsider our Case, and grant
us the same Indulgence which your Honour has been pleased
to allow the other Gentlemen in our situation, and which is so
absolutely necessary to our Private affairs." Thus Stephen De
Lancey, of Albany, charged with being notoriously inimical to
American liberty, with drinking " damnation to the Congress,"
with associating with the enemies of the country, " paying no
regard to circumstances or character," and with reporting to
Sir John Johnson the movements of the army and the debates
of the Albany Committee of Safety, *applies* for permission to
return home.

By this comparison with the official records in the case what
is left of the Judge's libel upon the State of Connecticut? The
records seem to have their own very positive reply, that not a
single statement in it is to be accepted as true.[1]

---

[1] The references to the resolutions of the Connecticut Legislature are from
Hinman, who produced them *verbatim*, from the original records in the Connecti-
cut State Library. The paroles are to be found in *Force's Archives*. Trumbull's
Papers contain the original duplicates.

VIII.—THE PENNSYLVANIA PROPRIETARY ESTATE.

Not much better fortune favors the "learned " Judge when he
proceeds to divulge and denounce the methods by which the
great proprietary province of Pennsylvania was transformed into
a republican State. It was no minor matter. "An extraordinary and surprising exertion of the power of Congress," he
writes, "shall be now related;" and we then have a statement
of the royal grant to William Penn of the vast tract of land
known as Pennsylvania, its revenues and patronage, the absolute rights of the proprietors and their heirs, and finally the ruth-
less change in the ownership and system brought about by the
Revolution. The points he desires to emphasize are as follows
(Vol. I. p. 327):

"In 1777, Congress, by a resolution of their own divested the Penn family of
all the powers of Government, and the liberties, privileges, and emoluments
granted them by the royal charter, without any compensation whatever, and converted the government from a kind of monarchy into an absolute republic, and
every office which was in the appointment of the proprietors, they made elective
and dependent upon the suffrages of the people at large. This, it seems, was not
sufficient, and Congress therefore in 1779, passed another resolution, by which
they divested the proprietors of all their quit-rents, with the whole of their unap-
propriated, unlocated, and unsettled lands in the province, of the value of at least
£500,000 sterling, and vested the same in the State of Pennsylvania, to be disposed of in such manner, and form, as the Legislature of that State should think
proper, for the benefit of the good people thereof. In doing this, however, they
looked upon themselves as bound in justice to make the family a compensation.
They accordingly resolved that the State should pay to the proprietors, in lieu of
their property (thus unjustly taken from them), the *amazing* sum of £130,000
sterling, to be paid in instalments without interest, and the first payment not to
commence till ten years after the end of the war. Was there ever a greater piece
of injustice, of villainy, or dishonesty than this ? Deprive a family of the powers
of government, of a patronage worth £70,000 per annum, without the least compensation, and of private property to the value of £500,000, in consideration of
£130,000, payable in instalments, without interest, and to commence ten years
after the war ? Thus did Congress, by an arbitrary, despotic, and assumed power,
reduce to indigence, and almost beggary, a family possessed under the Crown of
powers, privileges, emoluments, immunities, and a revenue, superior to half the
princes in Germany. Was this justice? Did the proprietors deserve this treatment from their hands ? Were any of the family consulted in this business?
They were not, Congress made their own bargain, Congress took away the estate,
and Congress stipulated the consideration money. If the proprietors ever get
£10,000 of the stipulated sum, they may think themselves well off. Congress

might, with as much propriety, have taken away all the unimproved and uncultivated land throughout the thirteen colonies, though granted by the Crown, and vested such lands in the several States in which they lay. Had this been done, much would not have been thought of the other. But to fall upon one family, and that a family of friends, too, dispossess them of their property, and leave all others in possession of theirs, is a species of such bare-faced partiality, villainy, and dishonesty, that no body of people, crowned head, or government (the American Congress excepted) were ever guilty of."

The three material statements in this extract are open to material corrections. *First*—it was not *Congress* that divested the Penn proprietaries of their estates. *Second*—the Legislature of Pennsylvania alone was responsible for the proceedings in the case, and presented solid reasons in justification of its course. *Third*—the Penn family retained a considerable property in Pennsylvania and in addition received the £130,000 consideration in full with interest, within six years after the war and three years before Judge Jones' death. The history of the case is briefly as follows:

Prior to the Revolution the Penn family claimed, under charter, to be sole owners of the province of Pennsylvania. Its government consisted of the hereditary Governor, his council and a General Assembly. In 1775 the latter body moved cautiously in dealing with the troubles with Great Britain, while the Governor opposed the colonial pretensions. The patriotic element in the Assembly and the population at large, recognizing the necessity of a more outspoken policy on the part of the State, organized a "Provincial Conference of Committees," which proceeded to open the way for a new government in accordance with a recommendation of the Continental Congress of May 18th, 1776. This recommendation was a general one, extended to all the States alike, and was prompted by an anxiety to suppress the exercise in America, of "all authority under the crown of Great Britain." The majority of the States were already represented by conventions or assemblies of the right cast, and on June 18th the Pennsylvania Conference, adopting the suggestion of Congress, brought themselves into line with their neighbors by resolving that the then existing government was "not competent" for the times, and that a provincial convention be called to form another government resting "*on the authority of the people only.*" Such a convention was soon organized, a new Constitution adopted September 28th, 1776, and the first General Assembly under it met on November 28th following. This was the extent of the local revolution in Pennsylvania in 1776, and it is difficult to question the propriety or necessity of the movement, as long as the right of revolution is recognized at all. The ownership of the soil was not then involved. At that date the Proprietary Governor, now without office, was John Penn, grandson of William Penn. " He remained," says Mr. W. B. Reed, " in Pennsylvania and appears to have been a temperate and inoffensive man, who relinquished his political authority without a struggle and was content to watch with unobtrusive vigilance the more substantial interests of his family."

More than two years elapsed before the special subject of the ownership of the soil came up in the Assembly. Congress made no recommendation in regard to it in 1776, and it made none now. *All the proceedings in the case were the voluntary action of the Pennsylvania Legislature.* The first we hear of the matter is in the message sent by the Executive Council through its President, Joseph Reed, to the Legislature on February 5th, 1779. " We shall now offer," says this document, " the last, though not the least object of your public enquiry and deliberation ; we mean the nature and extent of the claims or estates of the late proprietaries, and their consistency with the interests and happiness of the people under the late revolution. To reconcile the rights and demands of society with those of private justice and equity in this case, will be worthy your most serious attention." The Assembly took up the subject twelve days later, February 17th, and notified the late Governor, John Penn, of its intention to discuss it on the 26th of the same month. Mr. Penn thereupon requested the House not to take decisive action " until a reasonable time was allowed him to consider," and on March 10th and 11th it was voted that Penn as well as the State be heard by counsel, the House declaring itself " desirous of doing the strictest justice between the people of the State and the said late proprietaries." On the 18th and 22d the arguments were heard on both sides, but of these, as far as known, not even an outline is preserved. Before taking final action, the Assembly submitted several questions to Chief Justice McKean,

of the State Supreme Court, requesting his opinion on the
validity of the proprietors' claims from a legal point of view.
The answers, one point excepted, were in favor of Penn ; but the
Judge was particular to say that they were purely *legal* answers
and that the *political* situation had not been taken into account.
These questions and answers together with the report of a Committee of the Assembly, taking an opposite view, were ordered
to be printed both in English and German, so that the people
of the State were well informed of the action of their representatives in so important a matter. Finally on the 24th of November, 1779, an act was passed by the Assembly, known as the
" Divesting Act," by which the title to the soil of Pennsylvania
was virtually transferred from the Penn family into the hands of
the State. The vote in its favor stood forty to seven. John
Penn naturally protested against the act as "injurious and repug-
nant to every rule of justice and equity," and his protest was
allowed to be entered in the minutes of the Assembly.

This synopsis of the case, which is substantially the same as
that given by Mr. Reed, with a few additional data taken from
the Assembly's Journals,[1] at least settles the point that *Congress
was not concerned in it*, and that Judge Jones' denunciations of
that body are entirely misapplied. To reverse his finding in his
own words, Congress exercised *no* power, whether arbitrary,
despotic, or assumed, over the Penn family; did *not* reduce it
almost to beggary ; did *not* make its own bargain ; took away *no*
estates and stipulated *no* consideration money, and hence was
guilty neither of "partiality, villainy or dishonesty."

Whether the Pennsylvania Assembly must come in for the
condemnation intended for Congress is another question, and
perhaps not a question of fact. Judge Jones declares that a
glaring piece of robbery was committed somewhere by authority, and that the great majority of the people of Pennsylvania
are enjoying life to-day on stolen soil. The historical students
of that State would no doubt repel the insinuation, and could
probably find ample vindication of the action of the Assembly
of 1779. What the Judge asserts is in reality no more than his

---

[1] *Reed's Reed.* Vol. II , p. 166.   *Journals of Pennsylvania Assembly*, 1779.

conviction that the transfer of title was an act of robbery, while
the Assembly thought quite otherwise. The question is open
to argument, and as the Judge presents one view, the preamble
of the Act itself may be inserted here, as embodying the opposite
or Pennsylvania view:

"*An Act for Vesting the Estates of the late Proprietaries of Pennsylvania in this
Commonwealth.*

WHEREAS the charter from Charles the second, heretofore King of England, to
William Penn, under which the late province, now state of Pennsylvania was first
begun to be settled, was granted and held for the great ends of enlarging the
bounds of human society, and the cultivation and promotion of religion and
learning; and the rights of property and powers of government, thereby vested in
the said William Penn, and his heirs, were stipulated to be used and enjoyed, as
well for the benefit of the settlers as for his own particular emolument agreeable
to the terms of the said charter, and of certain conditions and concessions entered
into between them.

II. And whereas the claims heretofore made by the late Proprietaries to the
whole of the soil contained within the bounds of the said charter, and in consequence thereof the reservation of quit rents and purchase money upon all the
grants of lands within the said limits, cannot longer consist with the safety, liberty
and happiness of the good people of this commonwealth, who at the expense of
much blood and treasure, have bravely rescued themselves and their possessions
from the tyranny of Great Britain, and are now defending themselves from the
inroads of the savages.

III. And whereas the safety and happiness of the people is the fundamental law
of society, and it has been the practice and usage of states most celebrated for
freedom and wisdom to controul and abolish all claims of power and interest
inconsistent with their safety and welfare; and it being the right and duty of the
representatives of the people to assume the direction and management of such
interest and property as belongs to the community, or was designed for their
advantage.

IV. "*Be it therefore enacted, etc.*"

This preamble appears to be the only channel through which
the views of the Pennsylvania legislators of 1779 can now be
ascertained, but it contains enough to show that they put the
broadest construction upon the Penn charter, and felt that it was
intended to serve a *public* as well as a private purpose. They
seem to have held that the Penns were trustees of the province,

¹ *Laws of the Commonwealth of Pennsylvania.* By Alex. James Dallas.
Phila. 1797.

holding for the benefit of the settlers as much as for themselves, and that what the Revolution justified and the new form of government required was the transfer of the trusteeship from the family to the State. In this view they went beyond the technical opinion of Judge McKean, but perhaps came nearer to the intent of the original grantor.

Finally the property reserved to the Penns, whom the Judge leaves in absolute poverty, was large, though at that time probably unproductive. While the Divesting Act took from them what could properly be regarded as public lands, Section VIII. provided that all their private estates to which they were then entitled in their several right and capacity, and likewise "all the lands known by the name of the Proprietary Tenths or Manors" together with " the quit or other rents and arrearages of rents," reserved out of those manors which had been sold, should be confirmed to the family forever. It was, without doubt, to this property that Benjamin Franklin referred when he wrote in 1789, "The Penn estate is still immensely great."[1] To complete the settlement, the Act also provided that the sum of one hundred and thirty thousand pounds, sterling money of Great Britain, should be paid to the legatees of the Proprietaries, both as a mark of the State's liberality and its remembrance of the enterprising spirit which distinguished the founder of Pennsylvania, and also in order to provide for such pending marriage settlements and wills which otherwise would be defeated, to the loss and disappointment of the parties concerned. This money was duly paid in instalments, with interest, the last payment being made upon the order of the Supreme Executive Council on March 20th, 1789.[2]

---

[1] Letter in *Bigelow's Life of Franklin*, Vol. III., p. 448.
[2] *Minutes of the Supreme Executive Council of Pennsylvania*. Colonial Records, Vol. XVI., p. 53. See in this connection John Penn's Journal of a visit to some of his Pennsylvania estates in 1788, *Penn. Mag. of History*, Vol. III., No. 3, p. 284.

IX.—SCENES AT THE EVACUATION OF CHARLESTON AND SAVANNAH.

Another remarkable piece of history, treasured up by the Judge and now first brought to light, reflects terribly upon the conduct of the Americans upon the occasion of the final evacuation of the cities of Charleston and Savannah by the British in 1782. "Savagely cruel treatment of the loyalists at the evacuation of Charleston," is the reference to the case in the index. What the Judge reveals is as follows (Vol. II. p. 236):

"No sooner had the evacuation taken place at Charleston than the rebels, like so many furies, or rather devils, entered the town, and a scene ensued, the very repetition of which is shocking to the ears of humanity. The Loyalists were seized, hove into dungeons, prisons and other prevosts. Some were tied up and whipped, others were tarred and feathered; some were dragged to horse-ponds and drenched till near dead; others were carried about the town in carts, with labels upon their breasts and backs, with the word 'Tory' in capitals, written thereon. All the Loyalists were turned out of their houses, and obliged to sleep in the streets and fields, their covering the canopy of heaven. A universal plunder of the friends to government took place, and, to complete the scene, a gallows was erected upon the quay facing the harbor, and twenty-four reputable Loyalists hanged in sight of the British fleet, with the army and refugees on board. This account of the evacuation of Charleston I had from a British officer who was upon the spot, ashore at the time, and an eyewitness to the whole. No doubt the Loyalists upon the evacuation of Savannah shared the same fate with their brethren in South Carolina."

This is strong and positive, but it may be worth observing that, notwithstanding Judge Jones and his eye-witness, all the best evidence in the case published on either side leads to but one conclusion *that the occupation of Charleston and Savannah by the Americans in 1782 was effected with the utmost "order and regularity," and that no such scenes of violence, outrage, and plunder occurred.* It is to be questioned, indeed, whether there were any loyalists left in the two cities whose toryism was sufficiently pronounced and offensive to excite the alleged acts of retaliation. Many hundreds, it was known, had embarked with the enemy, and these presumably included all who had special reasons for dreading to remain. Advices from Charleston published in New York represented the whole number of persons who left Georgia in consequence of the evacuation of Savannah at nearly seven thousand, of whom five thousand were negroes, or more than three-fourths of all the slaves in the State. The two thousand whites included "almost all the wealthy inhabitants of the province, and many of the lower classes of the people." These figures may or may not be exaggerated, but that the exodus was large enough to warrant the suspicion that few of any consequence remained appears from the following schedule, preserved among the manuscripts of the Massachusetts Historical Society:

Return of People embarked from South Carolina and Georgia. Charlestown, 13th December, 1782.

From whence Embarked.	To what place.	Whites.			Blacks.	Total.
		Men.	Wom'n.	Child'n.		
Charlestown	Jamaica	600	300	378	2013	3891
	East Florida . .	630	306	337	1653	2926
	Do.	100	57	119	558	900
	England.	137	74	63	50	324
	Halifax.	163	133	121	53	470
	N. York	100	40	50	50	240
Georgia¹.	St. Lucia. .	20	. . . .		350	370
	Jamaica	50	. . . . . .	. . . . .	1600	1650
	E. Florida	320	159	236	1749	2500
		2142	1099	1304	8676	13271

But even admitting that prominent tories remained in both places, it is not to be admitted that they suffered the abuse described. Take Savannah, the town evacuated first, at noon, July 11. General Wayne commanded the American force then operating in Georgia. A few weeks before the enemy departed a deputation of tory refugees waited upon him to inquire whether, in case they remained, their "persons and properties" would be protected. The General replied briefly in writing :

"Should the Garrison eventually effect an Evacuation, the Persons and Properties of such Inhabitants, or others who chuse to remain in Savanna, will be protected by the Military, and resigned inviolate into the Hands of the Civil Authority of this State, which must ultimately decide.

Given at Head Quarters
June 17, 1782."²

¹ The figures opposite Georgia include only those persons from that State who happened to sail from Charleston, Dec. 13, and does not represent the total number who left the State from Savannah.

² *N. Y. Gazette*, Aug. 12, 1782, and other papers.

Taking possession of the place upon the enemy's departure, Wayne issued the following order to guard against the very excesses which Judge Jones believes to have occurred there. That the General's commands were literally obeyed no one familiar with his military record can doubt.

"HEADQUARTERS SAVANNAH, 11ᵗ July, 1782.

The light infantry company under Captain Parker to take post in the centre work in front of the town, placing sentries at the respective gateways and sally-ports, to prevent any person or persons going or entering the lines without written permits, until further orders.

No insults or depredations to be committed upon the persons or property of the inhabitants on any pretext whatever; the civil authority only will take cognizance of the criminals or defaulters belonging to the State, if any there be. . . .

N.B. Orders will be left with Captain Parker for the immediate admission of the Honorable Executive Council and the Honorable Members of the Legislature, with their officers and attendants." [1]

On the next day Wayne reported to General Greene in South Carolina as follows:

"HEAD QUARTERS SAVANNAH, July 12, 1782.

DEAR GENERAL

The British garrison evacuated this place yesterday at 12 o'clock leaving the works and town perfect, for which the inhabitants are much obliged to that humane officer Brig. Gen. Clarke . . . . I have further agreed that the merchants and traders not subjects of America, or owing allegiance to this State, should have six months allowed them to dispose of their goods and adjust their concerns, at the expiration of which term they should be furnished with a passport to transport themselves and property, received in exchange of payment of their goods, to one of the nearest British posts. I also agreed to receive all such citizens as had heretofore joined the enemy, on condition that they inlisted in the Georgia battalion of Continental troops to serve as soldiers for two years or during the war, in consequence of which, Major Habersham has already near two hundred men, and will shortly complete the corps without one farthing expense to the public . . . The Governor and Legislature meet here this evening or to-morrow into whose hands I shall resign the civil police." [2]

From these official letters and orders it appears that, upon the evacuation of Savannah, General Wayne immediately occupied the place in person with a detachment of Continental troops, that he issued stringent orders against every kind of insult or disorder, that he prevented the entrance or exit of irresponsible parties, that he granted very liberal terms to such

[1] *Stevens' History of Georgia,* and the newspapers of the day.
[2] *N. Y. Gazette,* Aug. 26, 1782.

British merchants as could not leave with their goods, and that the only condition he imposed on tories who had openly joined the enemy was their enlistment in the Continental army.[1]

Still more conclusive is the evidence in the case of Charleston, which was not evacuated until five months later, December 14, 1782. Lieutenant-General Leslie was in command of the enemy within the city. Major-General Greene, commanding the department of the South, and whom Wayne had now joined, lay encamped a few miles distant, awaiting Leslie's departure. Hostilities having practically ceased, it was agreed by the two commanders that the evacuation and occupation should be effected peaceably, for the security of the town and the safety of the inhabitants. The British accordingly embarked at leisure, the first detachment of the army going on board the transports at one o'clock P.M. on the 13th, the second at 3 P.M., the third at 7 A.M. the following day, and the last two hours later at 9 A.M. This order of embarkation in detail is preserved also among the papers of the Massachusetts Historical Society, the final paragraph being as follows:

" . . . . Second embarkation at nine o'clock the forenoon [Saturday, December 14th] consisting of the Rear Guard.

	Officers.	Men.	
Detachment of Artillery....	3	45	
Jagers.......	2	70	Gadson's Wharf.
Detachment 60th, 3d, and 4th Batt'n..	6	100	
63d Regiment....................	19	193	
Total.....................	30	468	
Total to embark this day...........	105	1290	
Total embarkation...	279	3848	

JNO. STAPLETON,
A. D. A. G'L."

[1] Major Alex. Roxburgh, of the Maryland line, writing to General Smallwood, from Camp Ashly Hill, S. C., July 14, 1782, says "The enemy have evacuated Savannah . . . The torys have all joined General Wayne, and have become American soldiers for the war, by way of atonement for their joining the enemy."—*Papers relating to the Maryland Line during the Revolution.* By Thos. Balch.

As this rear-guard withdrew from Charleston, the American light infantry marched in, with General Wayne at their head. Judge Jones compels his readers to imagine that officer permitting his men to enter the city like " so many furies, or rather devils," and conducting themselves in a shockingly inhuman manner! But Generals Greene, Moultrie, Horry and other officers, all present on the occasion and all the best of witnesses, give us accounts of the occupation, which, taken together and with published English accounts, render the Judge's version wholly inadmissible. In the first place we have Greene's report of the evacuation to the President of Congress as follows :

" HEAD QUARTERS, Dec. 19, 1782.

" I have the honour to communicate to your Excellency the agreeable information of the evacuation of Charlestown, and beg leave to congratulate you upon the event.

The enemy compleated their embarkation on the 14th, and the same day fell down into Rebellion road, and on the seventeenth crossed the bar and went to sea. It is said the Hessian troops are bound for New York and the British for the West India islands.

General Wayne, with the legion and light infantry (as general Gist was absent, and too unwell to continue his command) had been before the enemy's works for several days previous to the evacuation. General Leslie, by his adjutant general, hinted to General Wayne, through Mr. Morrice Simmons, one of the citizens of Charleston, his apprehensions that an attack from us might lay the town in ashes, and that if they were permitted to embark without interruption, every care should be taken for its preservation.

Knowing the impossibility of doing the enemy any material injury on their embarkation in a fortified town, and under cover of their shipping, and being well informed that some attempts had been made by some of the refugee followers of the British army before the place, I directed the general to make the safety of the town the first object, and that if a treaty was necessary for this purpose, to enter into one, rather than expose the place, for the little advantage which might be obtained over the rear-guard. The general, accordingly, from the intimation of the adjutant-general, very judiciously agreed to let them embark without molestation, they agreeing not to fire upon the town after getting on board.

" The conditions being understood by both parties, the town was evacuated and possessed without the least confusion, our advance following close upon their rear. The governor was conducted into his capital the same day, the civil police established the day following, and the day after the town opened for business . . .

Published by order of Congress,
CHARLES THOMPSON, Secretary."[1]

General Moultrie, in his well-known " Memoirs," enters more

fully into the details of the occupation. Thus, respecting Wayne's entrance into Charleston, he says :

"General Leslie who commanded in town sent a message to General Wayne, informing him, that he would next day leave town, and for the peace and security of the inhabitants and of the town, would propose to leave their advanced works next day at the firing of the morning gun; at which time General Wayne should move on slowly, and take possession; and from thence to follow the British troops into town, keeping at a respectful distance (say about two hundred yards;) and when the British troops after passing through the town gates, should file off to Gadsden's wharf, General Wayne was to proceed into town, *which was done with great order and regularity*, except now and then the British called to General Wayne that he was too fast upon them, which occasioned him to halt a little. About 11 o'clock, A. M., the American troops marched into town, and took post at the State-house."[1]

Moultrie then states that at three o'clock the same afternoon, General Greene, Governor Matthews, himself and others, with a few citizens and a guard of dragoons, rode into Charleston, and halted in Broad Street. "There we alighted," he continues, "and the cavalry discharged to quarters; afterwards every one went where they pleased ; some in viewing the town, others in visiting their friends." "I cannot forget," adds the General, "that happy day when we marched into Charlestown with the American troops ; it was a proud day to me, and I felt myself much elated at seeing the balconies, the doors and windows crowded with the patriotic fair, the aged citizens and others congratulating us on our return home, saying, 'God bless you, gentlemen! you are welcome home, gentlemen!' Both citizens and soldiers shed mutual tears of joy."

So also, Colonel Peter Horry, of Marion's brigade, who accompanied the advance corps into the city, describes somewhat fervently the scenes of the occasion, and the sensations he felt.

"On the memorable 14ᵗʰ of December, 1782," he writes, "we entered and took possession of our capital, after it had been two years seven months and two days in the hands of the enemy. The style of our entry was quite novel and romantic. On condition of not being molested while embarking, the British had offered to leave the town unhurt. Accordingly, at the firing of a signal gun in the morning, as agreed on, they quitted their advance works, near the town gate, while the Americans, moving on close in the rear, followed them all along through the city down to the water's edge, where they embarked on board their three hundred

---

[1] Moultrie's *Memoirs*, Vol. II. p. 359.

ships, which, moored out in the bay in the shape of an immense half moon, presented a most magnificent appearance.

The morning was as lovely as pure wintry air and cloudless sunbeams could render it, but rendered far lovelier still by our *procession*, if I may so call it, which was well calculated to awaken the most pleasurable feelings. In front were the humble remains of that proud army, which, one and thirty months ago, captured our city, and thence, in the drunkenness of victory, had hurled menaces and cruelties disgraceful to the British name. And close in the rear, was our band of patriots, bending forward with martial music and flying colors, to play the last joyful act in the drama of their country's deliverance, to proclaim liberty to the captive, to recall the smile on the cheek of sorrow, and to make the heart of the widow leap for joy. . . . . Oh! it was a day of jubilee indeed! a day of rejoicing never to be forgotten. Smiles and tears were on every face." [1]

Lieut.-Colonel Lewis Morris, of General Greene's staff, writing to his father, says briefly in regard to the evacuation : " This joyful event took place on the 14[3] Instant, and *a great regularity was observed by both parties*." [2] Major Alexander Garden, of the Legion, also leaves the impression in his "Anecdotes" that the city was occupied in a quiet and orderly manner. Still another eye-witness was Lieutenant Denny, of the Pennsylvania line, afterwards Adjutant-General of Harmar's Western army. Going into Charleston with the Governor, he had an excellent opportunity for making observations, and his testimony is important. He writes as follows in his journal under date of December 14, 1782 :

" Saw the last of the enemy embark in their boats, and put off to their shipping. An immense fleet lay in sight all day; *found the city very quiet—houses all shut up.* A detachment from the army had marched before to take possession as soon as the English would be off. *Guards stationed at proper places, and small parties conducted by an officer patrolled the streets.* Charleston, a handsome town, situate on neck of land between the confluence of Ashley and Cooper rivers; Cooper river, however, appears to be the only harbor. Town here fronts the east; business all done on this side. *Second and third day people began to open their houses and let themselves, and a few shops opened.* Stayed a week, and returned to our old encampment." [3]

Here we have the responsible eye-witnesses, Generals Greene and Moultrie, Colonels Horry and Lewis Morris, Major Garden and Lieutenant Denny, all separately reporting the perfect order

[1] *Horry's and Weems' Life of General Francis Marion*, p. 231.
[2] *N. Y. Historical Society Collections*, 1875, p. 500.
[3] *Major Denny's Journal in Memoirs of the Penn. Hist. Society*, Vol. III. p. 253.

attendant upon the occupation of Charleston when the British left it. Their joint negative testimony is significant. Not a single act of violence or disorder is referred to by them, and undoubtedly for the quite sufficient reason that none occurred. Add to all this the accounts given by the enemy themselves, and the conclusion is irresistible that Judge Jones' report is untrue from beginning to end. Thus in Rivington's New York *Gazette* for January 4, 1783, we have the following:

" The Honorable Lieutenant General Leslie, Commander-in-Chief of Charlestown, with his Suite, arrived here on Thursday in perfect health. . . . .

Immediately on the embarkation of the King's troops, at Charles-Town, the rebel General Wayne with about 5000 Continental Soldiers, took possession of the town, leaving a body of cavalry to guard the passes, with strict orders not to molest any person going to the shipping. The rebels were so extremely polite, after the embarkation of the garrison, as not to hoist the rebel standard for three days, while the English fleet lay in the Bay. . . . . We learn further, that when General Wayne took possession of Charles-Town, he ordered the houses that were shut up to be opened, *treated the inhabitants with civility*, and permitted them to carry on business as usual. That flags from the enemy had been received on board after the evacuation, that the treaty between the Governor and merchants had hitherto been inviolably held."

Again, in the Gazette of January 8, " some further particulars respecting the dereliction at Charlestown" are reported as follows:

" On Saturday the 14th ult. the business of evacuating Charlestown, the metropolis of South Carolina, was completed. The troops and stores having been previously embarked, his Majesty's ship Carolina, the Honourable Alexander Cochrane, Esq., Commander, which had been appointed to cover the embarkation, remained several hours very near the wharfs, after the British fleet had fallen down towards the Bar, and the rebel army taken possession of the town. Several parties of rebel cavalry and infantry paraded opposite to his Majesty's ship, but they neither offered nor received any insult. . . . . We hear, that before Charleston was evacuated it was insisted upon by the Hon. General Leslie and complied with by Mr. Green, that no corps of the country militia should be permitted to enter the town until the expiration of ten days after the British troops left it, by which time it was presumed that those merchants whose embarrassments compelled them to remain in the town, might get their property secured."

These several extracts speak for themselves, but hardly for Judge Jones. If the latter is correct, we must believe that Greene, Moultrie, Wayne, the Governor and others in authority, countenanced the grossest excesses, occurring under their eyes.

Of course they did not occur. The whole story, indeed, receives its quietus from *Rivington's Gazette*, which says nothing about those "twenty-four reputable loyalists" who were hanged in sight of the British fleet. Sir Alex. Cochrane, whose ship lay nearest the town, does not seem to have reported that interesting fact in New York ; nor did any one else on board the fleet mention the episode. This alone is sufficient to offset our contemporary Judge and his unnamed witness.

X.—THE NEW YORK ACT OF ATTAINDER.

As to this Act which the Judge brings forward as an illustration of the "injustice" and "dishonesty" of the Revolutionary legislature of the State of New York, it is to be said that no complete or *impartial* history of it can be written *so long as there does not exist on record a single line expressive of the views and motives of the men who framed and supported the Act.* We are absolutely in the dark as to the reasons and explanations given by the members of the Legislature to justify their votes in the case. Without this record any consideration of the Act must be unsatisfactory. Preeminently is Judge Jones' review of it unsatisfactory, as it is the review of one against whom the Act was to operate and whose facts and conclusions in other important matters have been found to be entirely worthless. One or two of his points, however, may be noticed.

In the first place, the Judge assumes to know precisely why he was included in the Bill as one of the enemies of the State whose person ought to be attainted and property confiscated, but without making it clear to the reader. On page 282-3, Vol. II., we are informed that it was because he ordered the discharge of four tories from jail in Westchester County, while holding Court there in the fall of 1775. "This official action was the reason given afterwards by a leading member of the House, to a friend of the Judge, why he was included in the Act of Attainder, &c." Again on page 304, at the close of his "Case" and elsewhere, he claims that his *adherence* to the enemy, charged in the Act, was nothing more than living upon his own estate on Long Island as a prisoner under parole. And finally he holds on pages 290-3 that he was attainted and proscribed on the charge of having broken his parole in not returning to Connecticut when called for by Governor Trumbull in the summer of 1777. The Judge insists that the New York Legislature did bring this charge against him, and then he endeavors to show that it was "a frivolous pretence only." But this is a charge not proven. There is no evidence whatever that New York took any notice of his presumed breach of parole to the Connecticut governor. In fact the letter of Governor Trumbull of March, 1780, to Governor Clinton, quoted *ante*, and Clinton's reply, go to show, rather, that the facts in the case were not generally known, and that the New York Legislators had no official data to guide them. The presumption is all the other way. If it has been shown that Governor Trumbull did not charge the Judge with a breach of his parole, it is wholly improbable that the Legislature of New York did. What the Judge states on the pages referred to, 290-3, thus seems to have no force or point.

The Act of Attainder says no more than that "divers persons," of whom the Judge was one, had been voluntarily adherent to the King with intent to subvert the liberties and government of the State, and that hence as a measure of public safety and justice their properties ought to be confiscated and themselves banished. As Judge Jones had defied or ignored the authority of the Provincial Convention in the summer of 1776; as he had been deemed dangerous enough to be arrested by Washington's order; as he voluntarily remained a prisoner under parole and by that very status proved himself an "adherent" to the enemy; and as he held property within the State of New York, whose government he wished to see overthrown, it is not difficult to understand how he came to be included in the Act of Attainder.

The further charge from the Judge that the Act was prompted by "malice, revenge and political resentment" is one which would naturally be made by him; but his proof is inconclusive. According to the Act only "the most notorious offenders" were included in the list. Selection was necessary. The State of Pennsylvania had already proceeded in the same manner, naming "divers traitors" for attainder. Delaware,

Georgia and South Carolina had their Confiscation Acts and lists of proscribed domestic enemies. The Act of Attainder passed by Parliament after the Scotch Rebellion of 1746, to which the Judge refers, included about eighty prominent individuals. In every case some choice had to be made. In the case of New York the matter was clearly a most delicate one, since the members of the Legislature had to deal largely with former political opponents. Some they dropped; others they included; and the Judge sees in this nothing but partiality, vindictiveness and villany. But all he has to offer in the way of proof is inference and speculation. He *knew* nothing about the matter. We need better informed witnesses before a verdict can be entered on this point of motives. The entire subject, to repeat, requires much more documentary light thrown upon it before it can be fairly and intelligently discussed. The Judge has treated it only from the standpoint of an avowed enemy.[1]

XI.—GOVERNOR TRYON AND THE CONNECTICUT RAID, 1779.

Passing within the enemy's lines, we find Judge Jones' hostility to Sir Henry Clinton, the British Commander-in-Chief, as deep-seated and bitter as it is towards the "rebels" and their revolution. The general's failure to suppress the latter is the explanation of the matter. Allowing for the moment that the Judge's delineation of Clinton has been drawn with an honest belief of its life-likeness and truth, and from purely disinterested motives, we must picture this British generalissimo as being a man without honor, without morals, without stability, morose in disposition, weak in his "intellects," a peculator while in high

[1] It would appear from the editor's preface that the Judge remained under the act of banishment as long as he lived, or otherwise he might have returned to this country. It appears, however, that in 1790 the Legislature passed a bill, Ayes 32, Nays 18, permitting him to return and remain here. The late Mr. O'Callaghan in a note in the *Historical Magazine*, 1858, Vol. II., p. 148-9, says "Though this Act is omitted by Greenleaf, it is on file in the office of the Secretary of State, Albany, and included the names of James Jauncy, Abraham C. Cuyler, William Smith, Wm. Axtell, *Thomas Jones*, Richard Floyd and Henry Floyd, the elder."

command, governed by a rebel spy, spurning good and true
loyalists, and as a military officer a mere incapable, utterly unfit
to be at the head of his Majesty's forces in America. The Judge,
in short, attacks Sir Harry at about every assailable point which
the human character presents. In particular, he ridicules his
military qualifications, and unsparingly criticises his entire military career.

It is not for the purpose of defending the British Commander-
in-Chief that attention is called to this rough handling he
receives from the author. It is simply the question over again,
Does Judge Jones sustain himself here, with any better success,
as a uniformly accurate narrator? The examination of a few
points may determine.

Take for example the events of 1779—Tryon's Connecticut
raid and the storming of Stony Point. The former movement
appears to have grated on the Judge's feelings so harshly that
relief could only come, as we may infer, by charging all the
burning, plundering and desecration committed by the British
at the towns of New Haven, Fairfield, and Norwalk directly
upon Clinton and his orders. The responsibility is fixed upon
him in person, and the officers in charge of the expedition
so far relieved of all blame. There is no uncertainty as to the
author's meaning and intent on this point.

" From the well-known humanity, charity and generosity of General Tryon,"
he writes (Vol. I. p. 315), " no man in his perfect senses can ever imagine that
the troops under his command were, with his consent, suffered to plunder peace-
able inhabitants, towns to be burnt, holy buildings destroyed, and thousands of
innocent inhabitants of both sexes, and all ages, and the greater part loyalists, to
be divested of all the comforts of life and turned into the open fields, no habita-
tions to protect them, exposed to the inclemency of the weather, and covered by
the canopy of heaven only. General Tryon's humanity was such that nothing but
express orders could have induced him to act a part so inconsistent with his well-
known and established principles. Clinton was at this time Commander-in-Chief."

It happens, however, that the unfavorable impression of Clinton which the Judge seeks to perpetuate in this extract, is entirely
dispelled by Tryon's own pen. Thus to Lord Germaine he wrote
July 28, 1779: " The honor of your Lord's duplicate dispatch
of the 5th May No. 21 afforded me the greatest satisfaction in the
King's approbation of my conduct on the Alert to Horse Neck.

It will be an additional comfort to me if my late expedition on the Coast of Connecticut meets the same royal testimony." As if to emphasize his own approval of the affair, he adds: " My opinions remain unchangeable respecting the utility of depradatory excursions. I think Rebellion must soon totter if those exertions *are reiterated and made to extremity."* Tryon in due time had the happiness to receive a favorable reply from the home government, and in returning his acknowledgments to Germaine, wrote Feb. 26, 1780: " I am honored with your Lordships Dispatches of the 4th Nov[r] and circular letter of the 4th Dec[r] and derive *great comfort* from His Majesty's gracious approbation of my conduct, and the officers under my command *on the Connecticut Expedition last summer."*

These few expressions on the part of the leader of the raid sufficiently answer Judge Jones as to the former's conduct and responsibility. The last official reference which Tryon seems to have made to the subject appears in the following note he sent to Governor Trumbull just before his departure for England:

"NEW YORK, 19th April, 1780.

[Duplicate.]

SIR, I take the opportunity by a Prisoner on Parole to send you a few of the Publications of this City, particularly the benevolent Proclamation of the Commander-in-Chief and my successor Governor Robertson, which when laid before your Council and Published in your Papers, may pave the way for a happy Reconciliation.

As General Robertson has succeeded me both in my civil and military command, *I shall probably not visit your coast any more,* but return to England the first favorable occasion to repair a Constitution much impaired in the service of my King and Country.

With my hearty wishes that the hour may be near at hand when the Prodigal children shall return to the Indulgent Parent,

I am
Sir,
Your Most Obe[dt] Servant,
WM. TRYON."[2]

N. Y. Colonial Do Vol. 8, p. 765.

Trumbull Papers, Mass. Hist. Society, Vol. XI., p. 144. Clinton's orders to Tryon before he left New York were produced for the first time in Capt. Chas. H. Townshend's pamphlet on the British invasion of New Haven, issued last year on the occasion of the centennial of that affair. These orders say nothing about burning of houses, plundering, etc., but simply authorize the destruction of shipping and stores, carrying off of cattle, and the employment of the expedition in distracting the "rebels."

XII.—SIR HENRY CLINTON AFTER THE STORMING OF STONY POINT.

The Judge makes a new and extraordinary statement in regard to Clinton's movements immediately upon his hearing of Wayne's Capture of Stony Point, July 16, 1779. The greater part of the British army at that date was encamped in the vicinity of Mamaroneck, close to the Connecticut border. It was Clinton's intention to make or support further demonstrations in that State in the hope of drawing Washington away from the Highlands to its protection. In that case an opportunity might offer of meeting him in the open field. But the re-capture of Stony Point by the Americans deranged these plans and compelled Clinton to move up the Hudson again to re-establish his posts there. Clinton's particular movements on and after the 16th of July are described as follows by the Judge :

While encamped in Westchester County near the Connecticut line, as stated, General Clinton, says the Judge (Vol. I. p. 312), " received an express acquainting him that the garrison at Stoney Point had been surprised, and made prisoners of, and conducted to the rebel army, and that the garrison at Verplanck's Point expected an attack every hour. Whether the General apprehended the city of New York in danger, or the garrison at Verplanck's Point of little consequence, no re-inforcements were sent to the latter. *The General marched with his whole army for New York,* all the hay makers with their covering parties, were called in. *The whole marched to Kingsbridge, passed the Harlem, and entered the island of New York. Most of them were quartered in the city. The remainder in its environs.* The lines at Kingsbridge in the meantime, were left to be defended by a refugee corps, some German Chasseurs, a few Anspachers, some British, and a few provincials, a motley crew consisting of not more than 1,000 men. Clinton established himself in the city of New York with about 20,000 men, a large body of militia, and a numerous train of artillery, and the island besides was surrounded by at least forty men-of-war. All this because Stoney Point had been surprised."

The Judge here puts it upon record as a matter of history, that General Clinton, who had moved forward expressly to operate upon Washington's flank and if possible draw him into an open engagement, became so thoroughly frightened at the news from Stony Point as to retreat precipitately, with all his men, to New York, where according to the author's own statement, made elsewhere, no defensive works existed, and there seek safety under the guns of his ships. But did this, or anything of the sort, occur? The correct records again authorize a denial of the entire statement.

In the first place, we have Clinton's own report in which he states that he marched to Stony Point as soon as he had the news of its loss. " *Upon the first intelligence of this matter,*" he writes, " *I ordered the army to advance to Dobbs' Ferry, pushing forward the Cavalry and some light troops to the banks of the Croton river, to awe the enemy in any attempt by land against Ver-plank's.* Brigadier-General Stirling was, in the meantime em-barked with the 42d, 63d and 64th regiments, for the relief of Verplank's, or the recovery of Stony Point. The northerly winds, rather uncommon at this season, opposed Brigadier-General Stirling's progress till the 19th; when, upon his arriving within sight of Stony Point, the enemy abandoned it with pre-cipitation, and some circumstances of disgrace."[1]

In the next place General Pattison, Commandant in New York City, reported substantially the same thing as follows: "Lieut.-Col. Webster maintained his ground [at Verplank's Point] with great spirit 'till the corps arrived under Brigadier-General Stirling, *which upon the first notice of the misfortune at Stony Point, was detached from Camp to support him.* Sir Henry Clinton at the same time moved the remainder of the army for-wards from Phillipsbourg to Dobbs' Ferry."[2]

Conclusive against Judge Jones as these two reports prove to be, ample confirmatory evidence is to be found in the manu-script dispatches of those American officers who commanded at the front, closely watching Clinton's movements. General Heath with the Connecticut Line had been detached to cover the roads leading from Mamaroneck. General Parsons was at Stamford, and General Wolcott, with Connecticut militia, at Horseneck. Parsons sent brief messages on the 16th and 17th to Heath with information that the enemy had not all retired from Mamaroneck. Wolcott reported on the 18th that his ac-counts satisfied him that at that date they had all gone " to-wards Hudson's River."[3] On the 19th, Heath at Mandeville sent word back to Wolcott: " The enemy have moved towards

[1] *London Gazette*, October 5th, 1779.
[2] *Pattison's Letter*, N. Y. Hist. Soc. Collections, 1875.
[3] *Heath Papers*, Mass. Hist. Soc.

King's ferry in Force." To Washington on the same date, he
wrote : " By intelligence received since I had the honor to
write in the morning, I learn that the enemy's advance sentinels
and videts were posted the last night on the New Bridge [Croton
River];"[1] and this is confirmed by Simcoe in his " Journals."
Finally on the 19th also, Wolcott writes a detailed account of
the enemy's movements, giving the names of the Corps and
where some of them quartered. The last troops, he reports, left
Mamaroneck "at 6 o'clock Saturday A. M. [the 17th]—The
17th Lt. Dragoons, the Legion, Simco, Rawdon's Volunteers
moved on the North Road to Phillipsburgh [the present
Yonkers], the others on the road to East Chester fileing off to
the Right and passing the Mile Square to the Same Place—
Genl. Tryon's troops landed at Frogs Neck and marched for
Phillipsburgh to join the Commander-in-chief. A young gentle-
man who returned from Phillipsburgh mentions the embarkation of Troops in the North River—the numbers he could not
tell. . . . General Parsons will easily apprehend thro what
channel this Intelligence is recd." This channel, it appears,
was one of General Parsons' friends, a Mr. Mornt, of Mamaroneck, who gave the information to N. Frink whom General
Wolcott had sent into the village for news.[2] The important
point in the report is the confirmation which "the young gentle-
man," Griffin, gives to Clinton's and Pattison's statement that
troops were embarked from Camp at Yonkers for Stony Point,
the moment its capture was reported.

Taking these several reports and messages, both British and
American, written in the field and at the time, and they justify
only one conclusion—that the entire British force in Westchester County moved forward and *not backward to New York*,
on and after July 16th, 1779. Did Judge Jones *see* the British
army crowded around the City at that date, that he so positively
assures posterity that Clinton acted the coward on the occasion?
No such sight could have greeted his eyes. He nevertheless
gives us the record of it which is as curious, absurd and false as
hearsay or imagination could make it.

[1] *Heath Papers*, Mass. Hist. Soc.
[2] *Wolcott Papers*, Vol. I. Conn. Hist. Society, Hartford.

XIII.—KNYPHAUSEN'S MOVE UPON WASHINGTON IN 1780.

Another effort to damage Clinton's record and make him out as worthless and incompetent as possible is made by the Judge in noticing movements in the vicinity of New York in the summer of 1780. In Vol. I. p. 355, he says:

"In the beginning of June, 1780, General Knyphausen, who was then Commander-in-Chief in New York, entered New Jersey at the head of an army consisting of several thousand men, determined to bring Washington to a general battle, or drive him out of the province. He proceeded as far as Springfield, about thirty miles from Elizabethtown, the place where the British army landed. Knyphausen was several times during his march attacked by the rebel militia, in conjunction with detachments from the Continental army. The rebels were always repulsed, and lost many men. The British lost some. Washington must have come to a battle, or given up the Colony. A fair battle was all the old German wanted. He now thought himself sure of it. But fortune favored Washington during the whole war. It now appeared in his favor again in a most conspicuous manner, for towards the latter end of the month, while the British and rebel armies in New Jersey were in the situation before described, General Clinton arrived from Carolina with 10,000 troops, and landed upon Staten Island. Whether Clinton thought Knyphausen would gain too much honor should he force Washington to battle, defeat him, and break up the rebel army, or by what other motives induced, is known only to himself and his privy council. He instantly upon his arrival, recalled the army from New Jersey, and ordered it to repair to Staten Island."

The impression the Judge desires to fix in the reader's mind here is that but for *Clinton's* untimely appearance and countermanding orders Knyphausen would in all probability have measured his strength with Washington, and driven him from the Jerseys. "A fair battle was all the old German wanted. He now thought himself sure of it." But the reader need not go far to ascertain that Knyphausen had *already* marched out, had his fighting, exhausted his movement, failed, retired and fortified himself at his starting point at Amboy, *full one week before Clinton arrived upon the scene.* The simple fact is that Knyphausen attempted, in Clinton's absence, to surprise Washington in his Camp at Morristown, but he met with so much resistance on the road from the Jersey militia that after getting as far as Springfield and finding a surprise out of the question, he wisely decided to turn back. The affair was reported to the home government by General Robertson in Knyphausen's name, in a

letter dated New York, July 1, 1780. "Under these circum
stances, [viz: the failure of the surprise and the number of
British wounded]" says Robertson, "General Knyphausen *gave
up the intention* of forcing Washington to an action in such an
advantageous post and resolved to wait in Jersey Sir Henry
Clinton's arrival, that he might be ready to act jointly or separately with him."[1]   Judge Jones' main point is thus disposed of
by the "old German" himself.   It was not *Clinton's* fault that he
was deprived of the honor of routing Washington.   That the
British commander was disappointed at the situation upon his
arrival from the South appears in one of his manuscript notes to
Stedman's History.   "This premature move in Jersey," he ob-
serves, "at a time when S. H. C. least expected it prevented a
combined movement against W. that might have been decisive."
In his published "Observations" on the same historian, he
makes further criticisms as follows:

"Mr. Stedman seems, in this account, to have followed American writers:
had he inquired, he would have found Sir H. Clinton did not arrive at New York
till after this expedition had taken place; that Sir H. Clinton knew nothing of this
anticipated movement (which, as he had not the least reason to expect it, he had
not forbid). If it had not taken place or could have been stopt in time by either
of the officers he had sent to prepare for one, in which he intended to have taken
a part with the corps he had purposely brought from Charlestown, success of
some importance might have been the consequence; as it was, every movement
that *did* take place after Sir H. Clinton's return to New York, was merely to
retire the corps, (which had moved into Jersey) without affront."[2]

After Knyphausen's *fiasco*, Washington, hearing of Clinton's
arrival from the South, moved toward the Hudson.   Clinton
then sent Knyphausen again into Jersey to ascertain the
American situation, and the unimportant battle of Springfield
was fought with Greene and our rear guard on June 23.   The
failure of this Jersey move must be laid upon the "Old German," Robertson and Tryon, not on Clinton, whose intended
plans they had disarranged.   Judge Jones, evidently, again did
not have facts before him when he wrote the above extract.

[1] *New York Colonial Docs.* Vol. VIII. p. 793.
[2] *Observations on Mr. Stedman's History of the American War.* By Lieut.-
Gen. Clinton, K.B.   London, 1794.   Fifty copies reprinted in New York, 1864.

XIV.—CLINTON, ARBUTHNOT AND ROCHAMBEAU, 1780.

On page 358, Vol. I., we have still another instance of Clinton's criminal indifference and incapacity as discovered by Judge Jones:

"In the summer of 1780," he writes, "a French fleet under the command of Monsieur De Ternay, with about 4000 men commanded by Monsieur Rochambeau, arrived at, and with the consent of Congress, took possession of, Rhode Island, having accidentally and luckily escaped the English squadron, then at sea under the command of Admiral Arbuthnot and in every point superior to the French. Arbuthnot, finding that De Ternay had eluded all the precautions he had taken to intercept him, and got safe to Rhode Island, returned to Sandy Hook." . . . . In a day or two the Admiral sailed for Rhode Island, blocked up the French fleet and then "sent an express to General Clinton, *proposing an attack as soon as possible upon the French fleet and army*, in Conjunction with the British army, who were to land and attack Monsieur Rochambeau, while the British fleet attacked that of the French. The French army were at this time but just arrived, were sickly, had erected no fortifications nor cast up any works worth mentioning. Clinton could have carried with him 12,000 men, without risking the safety of New York in the least. The success of the enterprise was undoubted. A noble achievement it would have been. Ten French men-of-war, with an Admiral's flag, either taken or destroyed, and a French army of 4,000 men, with an experienced General at their head, made prisoners of war. What answer was made to the proposal is uncertain. *Express after Express arrived from the Admiral, pressing the matter in the most urgent terms, and entreating the General to use the utmost despatch.*

"In about a month after the first express, Clinton ordered the transports up the Sound as far as Frog's Neck, about ten miles distant from his encampment on the North River. As soon as the transports arrived, he decamped, sent a part of his troops to New York, and with the remainder marched to Throg's Point, embarked, and sailed up the Sound. Great things were now expected; nothing less than the destruction of the French fleet, and the capture of Rochambeau and his army. But to the disappointment of every one, with a wind as fair for Rhode Island as it could blow, the whole fleet came to an anchor in Huntington Bay, about 30 miles to the eastward of Throg's Point, upon the Long Island shore. In this bay he continued as long as the wind remained fair (about a fortnight) for Rhode Island, where the enemy lay. As soon as the wind dropt about, and blew fair for New York, the signal was made, the anchors weighed, the sails unfurled, and to the mortification of every loyalist within the British lines the fleet moved to the westward."

In other words, we are to understand the Judge that it was *Arbuthnot*, and not Clinton, who projected this Expedition against the French, and that he alone was prompt and efficient, while the General played the laggard and caused the failure of the scheme.   But what says Clinton as to this in his "Observations" on Stedman?

"Sir H. Clinton, on receiving private information of the expected arrival of a French armament at Rhode Island, *proposed to Admiral Arbuthnot* (when he should be joined by Admiral Greaves) *that the French troops should be met at their landing*; for which purpose Sir H. Clinton was to have entered and landed in the Seconet Passage with 6000 men, covered by some frigates; and all that was requested of the Admiral was to block with his large ships the principal harbor, until any success the troops might meet with should induce the fleet to co-operate; but if the expedition should not take place before the French troops have been landed, and have repaired the works of Newport, and they should also have been reinforced, in that case Sir H. Clinton had given it as his humble opinion that the troops could not venture to act, unless the fleet would take an active part as well as the troops."

Not only did Clinton propose the attempt on the French, but he was the first to hear of their arrival. Writing to Germaine Aug. 14, he says: "On the 18th [July] by a courier from the East end of Long Island, the first intelligence was received of the arrival of the French off Rhode Island, on the 10th, which *I transmitted immediately to Admiral Arbuthnot.*" It was actually *ten* days after the French arrived before Arbuthnot appeared off Newport. *Five* days later only—the delay being caused by the non-arrival of transports which Clinton had ordered some weeks before—Clinton embarked from Throg's Neck under convoy of two war vessels from Arbuthnot's fleet, which joined him the day of his start, and proceeded to Huntington Bay. There, he reports, "*I was honored with such accounts from the Admiral, of the attention the enemy had given to fortify themselves,* that I no longer entertained an idea of making any attempt solely with the troops." [1]

In his own report to the Admiralty office, dated August 9, 1780, Arbuthnot makes no mention of any proposal on his part for a combined attack on the French, as Judge Jones asserts, nor that he repeatedly urged Clinton to join him with land forces. He did no more, after sailing around to Newport, than to report the situation to Clinton and leave the matter of his moving on with troops to the General's judgment. The Admiral's own words are conclusive: "In the meantime," he

---

[1] See both Clinton's and Arbuthnot's letters in *Almon's Remembrancer*, Vol. X. pp. 200, 204.

writes, "the Blonde and Galatea were left with orders to bring the transports under their convoy from New York *should the General judge an attempt on Rhode Island to be warrantable.*" What, then, becomes of the Judge's assertions that Arbuthnot was the man of the occasion, that Clinton delayed a month, that "express after express" was sent to him, and other misrepresentations to the same effect? What the Judge says further in regard to the General and Admiral is equally susceptible of disproof.

XV. — ADMIRAL PARKER, CLINTON AND FORT MOULTRIE, 1776.

Still another thrust at Clinton is made by the Judge in his account of the British attack on Fort Moultrie, Charleston harbor, in June, 1776. The lack of co-operation between the enemy's land and naval forces on that occasion has never been explained to entire satisfaction either by English or American historians probably because Clinton's own explanation in his "Observations" on Stedman had not been brought to their notice. As Judge Jones had not seen these "Observations," his own errors can be accounted for; but his treatment of the subject, nevertheless, is to be referred to as illustrating again with what alacrity he seized and recorded mere hearsay, rumor or plausible theory, if it furnished him an opportunity of turning it into a shaft at his enemies. His reference to the affair is as follows:

(Vol. I, p. 99) "During this long and heavy cannonade [by Admiral Parker's ships] the army, according to its projected plan, never made its appearance, nor did the Commander ever send word to the Admiral of his reasons for not co-operating with the fleet, the difficulties in its way, and its utter impracticability. This was inexcusable at least. The reason it seems was this: When the army marched, in order to carry their part of the plan into execution, they found the creek which divided the island instead of being knee deep to be not less than seven feet, and as they had neither boats nor bridge, the passage was impossible. This is the only reason that has been hitherto given and a surprising one it is. That a General should be nineteen days upon an island, was to carry on an attack upon another island adjacent, knew there was a creek to pass, *and yet in all that time had never disco[ve]red it, nor so much as found out its true depth of water!* This occasioned the failure of the attack, and of course all prospect of success in the Southern Colonies at that time. Was there ever a more stupid piece of business, except indeed when

5

the Ministry, after this, intrusted this man with the supreme command in North America, and the numberless stupid acts he did in that command?"

In his unpublished manuscript "Notes" on Stedman,[1] Clinton disposes of the Judge's version by stating that the depth of the water had been ascertained and report duly sent to Parker five days after the landing of the troops, or some twelve days before the attack was made.

"General Vaughan," continues Clinton, "who went to make this report to the Commodore, informed him at the same time, the troops could not act on that side, but offered him two Battalions to embark on board the fleet. Had this offer been accepted, the Commodore would have had sufficient force to take and keep possession of the fort, *if it had ever been evacuated*. The short fact is, the Commodore expected to succeed without the army; and perhaps, if he had placed his ships as near as he might have done, he would have succeeded; but at 800 yards distance, it was merely a Cannonade. The army could do nothing. Gen. Clinton received the King's approbation of his conduct. Had his letter been published, as well as that of the Commodore, no blame could have been imputed to the army. Certain queries of Gen. Clinton to Sir P. Parker, on reading his letter, and Sir P. Parker's answers, explain this whole business clearly. Perhaps the public may one day see them."

The "public" did see these queries and answers soon after, as Clinton published them in his "Observations." In his preliminary explanation the General says:

"It had been *finally* settled by Commodore Sir P. Parker and General Clinton, that part of the troops (there were boats for) were to have landed *not* on Sullivan's Island, as Mr. Stedman says, but on the main land, proceeding to it by creeks communicating with it; three of the frigates were to have co-operated with the troops in an intended attack upon Hedrall's Point, where the enemy had a work covering their bridge of communication with Sullivan's Island; the three frigates intended for co-operation with the troops, almost immediately run aground, in the hope they would soon float and proceed, the troops embarked on the 28th, and finding the frigates did not proceed, the troops of course disembarked, the same on the 29th, and as the frigates did not proceed, the troops could not."

The queries and answers are given as follows:

QUERE FIRST FROM GEN. CLINTON TO SIR P. PARKER.

"Did I not, very early after I had landed on Long Island, inform you, it was discovered that there was no ford at low water between Long Island and Sulivan's Island; and that I feared the troops could not co-operate in the manner we at first intended they should?"

---

[1] In the Carter Brown library, Providence, R. I. The extract here quoted is from Sparks' transcript of the "Notes" in the Library of Harvard College.

SIR C. PARKER'S ANSWER TO SIR H. CLINTON.

"You certainly made known your difficulties, and in your letter of the 18th June, you say, 'there is no ford, and that the Generals concurred with you in opinion, that the troops could not take the share in the intended attack they at first expected to do.'"

QUERE SECOND FROM GENERAL CLINTON TO SIR P. PARKER.

"Did I not offer two battalions to embark on board the fleet, and General Vaughan to command them, should you see any service in which they might be useful on your side?"

ANSWER.

"Some conversation passed between General Vaughan and myself about troops, but I did not think it material; and I was so extremely ill on my bed during the time, that I could not attend to it, and am therefore, obliged to refer you to General Vaughan for the particulars."

QUERE THIRD FROM GENERAL CLINTON TO SIR P. PARKER.

"Did I not request, that the three frigates might co-operate with the troops on their intended attack on the post of Hedrall's Point?"

ANSWER.

"The three frigates, besides performing the services mentioned in my public letter were intended to co-operate with you."

QUERE FOURTH FROM GENERAL CLINTON TO SIR P. PARKER.

"If the forts were silenced and evacuated for an hour and a half, was it the troops that were first to take possession (as Sir P. Parker's letter may seem to imply) or the sailors and marines, which Sir P. Parker informed Sir H. Clinton in his letter of the 25th June, *he* had practised for that purpose, that were first to land and take possession?"

ANSWER.

"I certainly did intend, as appears by my letter of 25th June, to have attempted taking possession of the fort with the sailors and marines first, but I could not have planned the doing of it with about 300 men, without the prospect of speedy support from you; and I saw, soon after the attack begun, from a variety of circumstances, you could take no effectual steps for that purpose."

Sir H. Clinton is persuaded there needs no comment on the above : if he should make any, it would be the two following short ones:

First, Had the frigates been able to proceed to their stations, an attempt (possibly a successful one) might have been made on the post of Hedrall's Point.

Secondly, If Commodore Sir P. Parker had accepted the General's offer of two battalions to embark on board the fleet, he would have had a sufficient force to take and keep possession of the fort on Sulivan's Island, *... that fort ever been silenced or evacuated.*[1]

In justice to Sir Henry Clinton, these explanations, giving his side of the story, should be made a more familiar matter of history. They appear to have proved an effectual answer to Stedman in 1794, and as satisfactorily answer Judge Jones to-day.

— — —

XVI.—FORTIFICATIONS OF NEW YORK. 1776-1783.

Among the various points of local interest upon which the Judge touches is the number of times New York City was fortified during the progress of the war. The editor of the work states in the preface, upon the authority of the Judge, that "the fortifications of New York were removed two or three times." The first defences were those constructed by the Americans in the spring and summer of 1776. What became of them after the city fell into the possession of the enemy is thus described by the Judge in Vol. I. p. 347:

" The General [Howe] by the advice of the principal engineer, his confidential friend [Captain Montressor], ordered all these forts, batteries, and redoubts, with two or three exceptions, with the barricadoes erected by the rebels, to be demolished, and the lines and entrenchments filled up and levelled. The performance of this business was committed to the care and direction of the aforesaid engineer, and to pull down what the rebels had erected at no expense, cost John Bull more than £150,000 sterling, £100,000 of which, the confidential friend put into his own pocket, returned to England, purchased one of the genteelest houses in Portland Place, a noble country-seat in Surrey, set up his carriages, had a house full of servants in rich livery, and lived in all the splendor of an Eastern prince. . . . In 1780 it was thought necessary (nobody, the Generals excepted, knew for what) to rebuild all the demolished forts that had been built by the rebels upon New York Island, and to add a number of new ones. This was done, the work was performed, that is the labouring part, by the inhabitants of New York. The General also thought it necessary (for his own safety no doubt, as no one else apprehended any danger) to have beacons erected all round the island, a circumference of at least 30 miles, and upon every hill, mount, or eminence, upon the island. Not less than 300 of the beacons were erected, with a tar barrel upon,

[1] Italics, Clinton's. Commodore Parker reported that during the progress of the bombardment the Americans evacuated the fort and left it unmanned for an hour and a half, which was not the case, however.

and a guard to each, to give timely notice of the approach of an enemy. In this business another £150,000 was expended, and another engineer returned to England in possession of his plum."

Add to these figures £100,000 alleged to have been expended upon works erected in Brooklyn in 1779, and £300,000 in 1781–82, and we have the sum of over £700,000 drawn from the treasury of Great Britain to pay for putting up and pulling down defences around New York during the war. The Judge may be correct. He makes his statements with the positiveness of a writer who has the treasury accounts before him. Certain points, however, require explanation—not respecting the figures but the defences. Is it a fact, for instance, that the New York works of 1776 *were* destroyed by the British, as the Judge asserts? The force of his statements depends on this, for if there was no tearing down there could have been little rebuilding and few "plums" for engineers. Eye-witnesses leave a brief record in the case. The English traveller Smythe, afterwards an officer in the service, reached New York on March 18, 1777. "I immediately," he writes, "visited all the posts in the vicinity of New York occupied by the British troops, and viewed *the multitude of works all over the island thrown up by the rebels,* which will remain lasting monuments of American folly and fearfulness." "To describe," he says elsewhere, "the works thrown up by the Americans upon this island would take up more room than this volume can afford, or the subject deserves, as they actually cover the whole island. Two only I shall take notice of, viz., a strong work on an eminence, just at the entrance into the town from the land which is named Bunker Hill, and the other is Fort Washington, &c." It seems from this that six months after the British occupation, the American works were still standing. How was it nearly a year after? Another English subject, Mr. Thomas Eddis,[1] lately a civil officer of the Crown in Maryland, wrote from New York on August 16, 1777: "The numerous fortifications thrown up by the American troops in the vicinity of the Capital, appear to be constructed with judgment and attention. Why they were so precipitately abandoned is difficult to ascertain: *indeed the whole*

---

[1] *Letters from America,* Thos. Eddis, p. 429.

*island forms a continued chain of batteries and intrenchments
which seemed to indicate the most resolute opposition."* Smythe
and Eddis not only examined the works in person but were
impressed with their great extent; and when Eddis wrote, *Sir
William Howe and his engineer Montressor were in Pennsylvania,
where they remained until superseded.* How much credit, then,
is to be given to Judge Jones when he tells us that all these
works were levelled, and that too under the "care" and "direction" of Montressor; and what becomes of the £100,000 he
pocketed for levelling what clearly never was levelled during
his stay in New York?[1]

References to the defences in the later years of the war,
though meagre, sustain the Judge but little better. In 1779,
when Sir Henry Clinton was preparing for his expedition against
Charleston, South Carolina, he proposed to leave New York safe
against the attack of the expected French fleet and forces. To
Lord Germain he wrote August 21: "I am therefore employing
the army to perfect the defences of this post, which at all events
must be left out of reach of any insult." But according to the
Judge there were, at that date, no defences to "perfect." Lieut.
Auburey wrote from New York, *October* 30, 1781, that the
American works "are not only on grounds and situations that
are extremely advantageous and commanding, but works of great
strength;" and in the "Political Magazine" for November, 1781,
there is a description of the city given in which the writer says,
that "Just without New York the Rebel redoubts and lines that
stretched from the East to the North River *still remain,* but
they are greatly decayed." The final and corroborative, or more
properly, the best evidence in the case, however, is that furnished
by the only known original map of New York City which shows
the defences erected by both sides during the Revolution,
namely, the map of the Engineer Hills, surveyed in 1782 and
drawn in 1785, deposited in the map room in the City Hall. In
the right hand corner, Hills entered three important explanatory

----

[1] It is true that the *Brooklyn* works were demolished by Howe's orders, but they
were but a small part of the whole, and the proof is yet to be produced that Montressor advised their demolition or pocketed any "plums." It would be interesting also to have something further about the 300 beacons around New York Island,
and the nightly detail of guards, involving at least 900 men, to light them!

memoranda as follows: "All the works colored Yellow were erected by the Forces of the United States in 1776.—Those works colored Orange were erected by Do and repaired by the British Forces.—Those works colored Green were erected by the British Forces during the war." According to this, if Judge Jones be correct, there should be at least one if not two distinct green-colored lines of works, protecting New York, on Hill's map. They may be searched for in vain. The American line is there with only such alterations and additions as the more skilful British engineers may have suggested or the varying exigencies of the situation during the long war required. Neither this map nor the contemporary writers quoted, give the least countenance to the sweeping assertions made by the Judge. Curiously enough the original American circular redoubt on the hill *on the Judge's own grounds* east of the Bowery remains on Hills' map still the same American yellow-colored circular redoubt (possibly repaired), and not a twice-rebuilt British battery, standing as a disgrace to peculating engineers!'

XVII.—THE CASE OF GENERAL WOODHULL.

The facts that General Nathaniel Woodhull, of Mastick, L. I., was President of the New York Convention when hostilities opened that he was in command of the Long Island militia at the time of the Battle of Long Island on August 27th, 1776— that he was made prisoner on the following evening—that he

---

' The editor of Jones' work states in the preface that the last works erected by Clinton "are those shown on the only map of the fortifications of New York in existence, that made by Hill in 1782, which are unfortunately often but erroneously supposed to be the American works of 1776, and have *even been reproduced as such very recently.*" This criticism could hardly have been made after an inspection of the original Hills in the City Hall. Under which description will Clinton's "last" works come,—yellow, orange or green? Nor is it stated what the erroneous map is that has been "recently" issued. The present writer perhaps may be permitted to say that, as to this, the most recently published map representing the defences of New York, so far as he is aware, is that accompanying Vol. III. of the Long Island Historical Society Series, which was compiled with care from the original Hills and followed the "yellow" line in locating the American works. This explanation appears in Part I. of that work, p. 84, n.

received dangerous wounds at the time of his capture from the effects of which he died on September 20th—and that some uncertainty and mystery attaches to the circumstances under which the wounds were inflicted, have excited the special interest of a number of historical writers, and provoked a discussion among them.

The point of controversy in the case, until Judge Jones' version appeared, related to the responsibility of one of the officers of the detachment which captured the General—the officer in question being Captain Oliver de Lancey, who was related to the Judge by marriage. It has been charged on one side that he struck Woodhull immediately after his surrender without sufficient provocation, and that his men thereafter continued to cruelly hack him about the head and arm. On the other side it is made to appear that, if Captain de Lancey took any part in the occurrence, it was to interfere and protect the General from further mutilation by the soldiers. The discussion was carried on by published correspondence in 1848 principally by J. Fennimore Cooper, Henry C. Van Schaack, Lorenzo Sabine, and Henry Onderdonk, Jr.

Judge Jones' narrative, however, puts the case on a new footing by alleging that General Woodhull received his wounds *while endeavoring to make his escape* subsequent to his surrender, in which case the wounds were justifiably inflicted by the soldier on guard. This view of the case was substantially endorsed by Fennimore Cooper, who quoted from the Judge's manuscript during the discussion referred to, and who, being, like the Judge, also related to the de Lancey family, naturally defended Captain de Lancey from the charge of cruelty in the Woodhull affair. Judge Jones is furthermore endorsed by the editor of his work, who claims that his account " has an authenticity that no other of the various versions of this occurrence can possibly possess." The whole matter thus turns upon the value of the Judge's testimony, and in this light only is it referred to here. Does Judge Jones *settle* the disputed point as *the* authority in the case?

It is claimed for the Judge that he was connected with the families of Captain de Lancey and General Woodhull, that he was personally acquainted with both, that he lived on Long

Island not many miles from the scene of Woodhull's capture, that he had ample opportunity to learn the particulars of the capture, and could not be mistaken in his account. " It will be seen," says Mr. Cooper in one of his letters in the controversy, " that from connection, residence, and social position, the historian [Jones] was every way fitted for his task. It was next to impossible that he should not have heard the story and its contradiction, and that undertaking to leave behind him a written account of the occurrences, he should have not used the means he possessed to learn the truth."

If this method of deduction, that because Judge Jones was *in the way* of knowing, he, therefore, *must* have known the truth in the case, is to be accepted, the door is opened for the introduction of an indefinite number of doubts and queries. The Judge was a prisoner in Connecticut at the time of Woodhull's capture, and did not return to his home until more than three months after the event. There is no evidence that any story was current at that time within the enemy's lines that Captain de Lancey was concerned in the General's death, and there was no necessity for its contradiction. If he was concerned in it, we cannot suppose that he would allow any such report to circulate, or that his friends would believe it. If the Judge, then, wrote his account without ever having heard of the charge against the Captain, he could have recorded only what he heard from others, the friends of the Captain, which in any view would have been favorable to the Captain. On the other hand, had the Judge heard of the charge, as Mr. Cooper believed " it was next to impossible" that he should not have heard of it, and at the same time knew that it was false, can there be any doubt but that he would have seized the opportunity to denounce the story as a scandalous " rebel" falsehood, and brought forward all the proofs in substantiation of his own version? But he does nothing of the sort, and we are left to infer that he recorded, as he does in so many other cases, simply what he had heard from others, which may have been the most acceptable of one of several current accounts.

But in addition, the elements of improbability are to be found in the Judge's version itself. His words are (Vol. II. p. 332):

"It may, from this state of the case, be naturally asked, how the General came to be so desperately wounded as to die of those wounds a few days afterwards? The fact is shortly this. The General, after his surrender, favored by the darkness of the night, attempted to make his escape, but being discovered by the sentries while attempting to get over a board fence, he received several strokes from their broad swords, particularly one upon the arm. He was carried on board a Man-of-War and treated with hospitality. The Surgeons advised amputation. To this he would not consent. The wound mortified and he died in a few days."

It is to be noticed that in this account we hear for the first time that Woodhull did not receive his wounds in connection with his capture. The Judge includes two distinct acts in the occurrence; *first*—the General was taken prisoner and guarded by sentries; *second* subsequently he attempted to escape but failed and was wounded in the attempt. Now this version conflicts with what the editor of the work describes as "the only two sworn accounts of the incidents of the Capture that exist." The first account comes through one William Warne who testifies that he was on Long Island after the Battle and that, among other pieces of information he had, "one of the light horsemen told *he had taken Gen. Woodhull* in the dark in a barn; that before he would answer when he spoke to the General, he had cut him on the head and both arms." The second comes from Lieut. Robert Troup who made affidavit for the information of the New York Committee of Safety, that he saw General Woodhull after his capture and was told by him that he was struck by his captors immediately after delivering up his sword. These two sworn Statements agree at least on the point that the General was wounded *at the time he was taken*—that he was not completely in the hands of the enemy until after he had been hacked and bruised; and this is the account given by the Long Island writers, Messrs. Wood, Onderdonk and Thompson (the latter a blood-relative of Woodhull), who took pains to examine the subject.[1] There is not anywhere, until Judge Jones' publication appeared, the slightest hint given that Woodhull endeavored to escape. Such an attempt would assuredly have been noised about by the enemy in self-justification.

To accept the Judge's account, we are thus compelled to

---

[1] It should be stated that Mr. Onderdonk also makes this point that Woodhull was clearly captured and wounded at the same time.

throw out all the prior and only "sworn accounts" in existence. They make the capture and wounding of General Woodhull *co-incident acts*, the one accompanying the other. Judge Jones makes them separate acts, and by this means would have Wood-hull become responsible himself for the injuries he received. All the accounts at best are second-hand accounts, but of the earlier ones it is to be noted that Warne received his version from a participator in the capture and Troup *from General Woodhull himself*. Upon all principles of evidence the affidavits of Warne and Troup are entitled to more credit than the unsupported statement of Judge Jones who does not inform us upon what authority he wrote, and who wrote as one in the de Lancey interest. In this view of the case, then, does the Judge clear up the Woodhull mystery? Is his account final and authoritative? Is there not good ground for the answer that the case remains where it was, with the weight of probability in favor of the *original accounts*, which represent that the General was wounded *at the time of his capture*, and that he made no attempt to escape?[1]

XVIII.—WASHINGTON AND CAPTAIN ASGILL.

The last of the Judge's statements which it is proposed to notice in these pages is the only remaining charge which he brings against the American Commander-in-Chief—the other three having been reviewed in Cases II. and V. In the present instance we have an account of the treatment which the British Captain Asgill is alleged to have received from Washington in

---

[1] Mr. Cooper endeavored to explain away or break down Troup's affidavit when he found it contradicting his own and the Judge's theories of the affair. The editor of the work appears to commit himself no further than to state that Troup was "certainly wrong" in saying that Woodhull perished, as he was informed, through want of "care and necessaries," Judge Hobart's letter of Oct. 7, 1776, being given as proof that Woodhull's wife was present *taking care of him* at the time of his death. But Hobart's words scarcely admit of such a free interpretation, for he says, significantly, that the General "was attended *in his dying moments* by his lady," clearly implying that she arrived too late to be of service, and was with him only at his death-bed. Hobart's and Troup's statements are easily reconcilable with each other.

1782, and which the Judge denounces in unmeasured terms. The Chief, indeed, is held up in the light of an uncivilized monster.

As a full review of the case would require many pages, attention is confined here to the most damaging part of the charge which reflects on Washington's humanity. To state the point briefly, Captain Charles Asgill, of the British Guards, then one of the prisoners in our hands, was designated by lot, as a victim for retaliation, to atone for the murder, by the enemy, of an American Captain, named Joshua Huddy, of Monmouth, New Jersey. In the eyes of Washington and all his principal officers, the peculiarly aggravating circumstances attending the death of Huddy justified this extreme method of obtaining satisfaction, especially as the British refused to punish the guilty parties within their own lines. Washington characterized Huddy's fate as "a crime of the blackest dye, not to be justified by the practices of war and unknown at this day amongst civilized nations;" and Sir Henry Clinton, when he heard of the particulars, also described it as an act of atrocity "scarcely to be paralleled in history." After the choice fell upon Asgill he was removed to the camp of the New Jersey troops at Morristown where Colonel Dayton commanded. It was while the Captain was awaiting the order of execution here that Judge Jones charges he received most outrageous treatment at the hands of the Americans.

"Captain Asgill," says the Judge (Vol. II. p. 232), "was not permitted to come into the presence of Washington [Washington was at a distance with the main camp near the Highlands, J.], but instantly put into a prison, deprived the liberty of pen, ink and paper, his servant refused admittance to him, and the diet allowed him bread and water, with once a week a scanty allowance of animal food. This bespeaks the humanity, the politeness, the virtue of Washington. Captain Asgill had but one window in his apartment, out of which he could peep at the sun, or draw in fresh air. To punish the unhappy youth as much as possible, the rebel chief ordered a gallows erected, 30 feet high, directly in front of, and at a small distance from the window, with this inscription in capitals, ' Erected for the Execution of Captain Asgill.' This gallows and this inscription presented themselves to the Captain's eyes whenever he approached the window, which for the benefit of fresh air must have been often. This was murdering a man by inches. It was a piece of barbarity that none but a rebel could be guilty of. Instant execution would soon have put the youth out of his pain, it would have been lenity, mercy, kindness, nay, it would have been generosity. Instead of suffering one death by an immediate execution, the unhappy young soldier must, in contemplation, have experienced one every day. Every morning that he arose, he naturally supposed was the last of his existence. He never looked out of his window but he saw the tremendous instrument of death, with the more tremendous inscription, 'For the Execution of Captain Asgill.'

"At conduct like this all Christians must shudder and execrate the unfeeling severity which could be guilty of so deliberate and wanton an act of cruelty."

The records fail to bear out this extraordinary story, but point directly to the opposite conclusion, that Captain Asgill received *no such treatment as here represented.* It was reported, for instance, after the war, that Asgill, who had been released, circulated some such story as the above himself in London, and the report was brought to Washington's ears. In reply to a friend who sought for information in the case, the Chief wrote as follows from Mount Vernon on June 5th, 1786:

"That a calumny of this kind had been reported I know. I had laid my account for the calumnies of anonymous scribblers but I never had conceived before that such a one as is related, could have originated with, or met the countenance of Captain Asgill, whose situation often filled me with the keenest anguish. I felt for him on many accounts, and not the least, when reviewing him as a man of honor and sentiment . . . . My favourable opinion of him, however, is forfeited, if being acquainted with these reports, he did not immediately contradict them. That I could not have given countenance to the insults, which he says were offered to his person, especially the groveling one of erecting a gibbet before his prison window, will, I expect, readily be believed, *when I expect . . . . and that I . . . .*"

Colonel Humphreys, formerly one of Washington's aids, published all the documents relating to the affair, so far as they could be found in the Head Quarters correspondence, and in his preface has the following paragraph :

"When I was in England, last winter, I heard suggestions that the treatment Capt. Asgill experienced during his confinement was unnecessarily rigorous, and as such reflected discredit on the Americans. Having myself belonged to the family of the Commander in-Chief, at that period, and having been acquainted with the minutest circumstance relative to that unpleasant affair, *I had no hesitation in utterly . . . .*"

Humphreys to the Editors of the *N. . Haven Ga. . .*, Nov. 6th, 1786. The correspondence was reprinted in pamphlet form for the "Holland Club," New York, in 1859.

Surgeon Thacher, who was also with the army at that time, gives many particulars of the case, and in a note on page 384, of his " Military Journal," after noticing exaggerated French accounts, writes:

"I can with the fullest confidence affirm, *that a gibbet never was erected for Captain Asgill at any period of his confinement,* and that no preparations whatever were made for his execution, except a secure confinement for a short period, during which the utmost tenderness and polite civilities were bestowed on him, and for these he expressed his grateful acknowledgments in his letter to General Washington. It would be preposterous to suppose, that the Commander-in-Chief could act a farcical part by exhibiting the machines of death, when it was altogether problematical whether an execution would be the final result, and surely nothing could be less characteristic of Washington, than wantonly to torture the feelings of a prisoner with the horrors of death."

Another important piece of evidence relating to the affair is that furnished by Major Alexander Garden, of Lee's Legion, in his well known " Anecdotes." He, also, speaks of these later reports and " abuse" lavishly disseminated by " the British Gazettes," and expresses himself as having been greatly surprised at and loath to believe them.

"I had been a school-fellow," he states, " of Sir Charles Asgill, an inmate of the same boarding-house for several years, and a disposition more mild, gentle, and affectionate, I never met with. I considered him as possessed of that high sense of honor, which characterizes the youths of Westminster in a pre-eminent degree. Conversing sometime afterwards with Mr. Henry Middleton, of Suffolk, Great Britain, and inquiring, if it was possible that Sir Charles Asgill, could so far forget his obligations to a generous enemy, as to return his kindness with abuse. Mr. Middleton, who had been our cotemporary at school, and who had kept up a degree of intimacy with Sir Charles, denied the justice of the accusation, and declared, that the person charged with an act so base, *not only spoke with gratitude of the conduct of General Washington, but was lavish in his commendations of Colonel Drayton, and of all the officers of the Continental army, whose duty had occasionally introduced them to his acquaintance.*"

Under this evidence it is difficult to find any confirmation of the Judge's version. He appears to have taken the newspaper stories of the time and converted them into historical fact. Captain Asgill was undoubtedly treated, as Washington directed Colonel Dayton, with the utmost indulgence. It was necessary to have him under strict guard but at the same time, wrote Washington to Dayton, " I must beg that you will be pleased to treat Captain Asgill *with every tender attention and politeness* (consistent with his present situation) which his rank, fortune, and connections, together with his unfortunate state, demands," To believe Judge Jones, we must assume that a noted Continental officer like Colonel Dayton deliberately disregarded Washington's instructions and allowed his prisoner to be insulted in the manner alleged an assumption which is not to be entertained. The whole gibbet and cruelty story must be relegated, with all the errors and libels already noticed, to the stock of myths from which the loyalist historian drew so freely.

XIX.—CONCLUDING POINTS AND OBSERVATIONS.

The foregoing cases, to which attention has been invited, are adduced as *instances* of erroneous statements to be found in Judge Jones' work, and not as the total of such errors by which the value of the history is to be determined. An exhaustive examination of all that the Judge assumes to contribute as new material upon the subject an examination which would require a search among unpublished records both in this country and Great Britain—would without question uncover further blunders of a similar character. There are statements made by the Judge, indeed, which ought to be rejected without call for disproof rejected upon their obvious improbability.

Nor are the errors noticed to be regarded as secondary matters, incidental, to be accounted for, and such as all historical writers are liable to fall into without impairing the value of their work as a whole. No such modifying criticism can be properly admitted. They are all *important, leading statements* with which the Judge clearly intended to make an impression. Eliminate them from his narrative, and it loses some of its strongest points; the indictment is deprived of a score or more of its main props. The Case of General Washington is in point; in regard to whom the Judge makes the four damaging statements that he once broke his own parole, that he countenanced the violation of the Judge's parole, that he favored the cruel abuse of tories, and developed the traits of a brute in his treatment of Captain Asgill. These matters are dwelt upon and emphasized by the Judge in order to stigmatize the memory of the Commander-in-Chief of the American "rebellion." But these charges have been found to be gross and untrue in all particulars. All the other references are equally surprising as developments of secret history, but they severally disappear by comparison with better records. The reader of the work cannot but be impressed with the fact that the Judge depended much upon the statements noticed *to make out his case* against the Revolution and his enemies generally. They enter as test illustrations in his line of argument, which becomes seriously weakened by their proven falsity and inapplication.

If, in addition, errors of lesser importance can be cited as affecting the credibility of a writer, the Judge's production is open to a more extended criticism. His work contains numerous minor mis-statements, showing either that he wrote carelessly or, what is much more probable, was without authentic sources of information. For example, his inaccuracies in giving figures, strength of forces, etc., are frequent; such as 10,000 American prisoners in New York at the close of 1776, when there were not 5000. He decries the raid upon the Connecticut coast in 1779, because New Haven, Fairfield and Norwalk were tory towns, "at least two-thirds of the inhabitants" of which were Episcopalians, and the greater part of whom "favored the royal cause during the rebellion." But as to New Haven, it may be said that she was regarded in Connecticut as a true Revolutionary town, and statistics show that the proportion of Episcopalians was less than one-twelfth of the whole.[1] It is also stated that during this raid Yale College "was

---

[1] New Haven in 1774 had about 6000 inhabitants. In Dr. Beardsley's *History of the Episcopal Church in Connecticut*, a letter from the Episcopal clergyman of New Haven, dated April, 1772, says "The souls, white and black, belonging to the Church in New Haven are 503; and in my church at West Haven there are 220." During the war the population diminished, and on Jan. 1, 1782, it stood, according to President Stiles' diary, as follows:

"Jan. 1, 1782. N. Haven had 3322 inhabitants.

Rev. Mr. Whittlesey	900	Congregational.
Rev. Mr. Eden	800	
Rev. Mather	950	
R. Hubbard	250	Episcopal.
Besides Yale College	220	

3120"

plundered of a library consisting of many thousand books which
had been collecting for very near 100 years, with many curious
and valuable manuscripts, a remarkably fine orrery, a celestial
and a terrestrial globe, and many other things of consequence;
besides a selection of well-chosen books, a present to that
seminary from the late Dean Berkley, afterwards Bishop of
Cloyne in Ireland, and known by the name of "The Dean's
Library." This, however, is all a gratuitous bit of history, for
Yale College was plundered of *nothing* by the British either on
that or any other occasion, losing neither books, manuscripts,
orrery or globe—a fact easily substantiated by reference to that
institution. The Judge, again, is shocked at the conduct of the
Americans in firing upon the funeral procession attending the
burial of General Fraser at Saratoga in 1777. "Had an act like
this," he says, "been committed by Britons, it would have been
trumpeted to the world as an act of the most savage barbarity, and
contrary to the laws and customs of all civilized nations, but being
performed by Americans, who boasted of fighting the battles of the
Lord, and contending for the rights of mankind, it was a righteous
act, and thought nothing of." The Judge had Gordon before
him and quotes him as giving the same account of the firing; but
he has not the candor to state, what Gordon does, that had the
Americans *known* that the party fired at was a funeral gathering
the cannonade would have been stopped. Upon this point
Madame Reidesel, wife of the German General in Burgoyne's
army, writes in her "Memoirs": "The American general, Gates,
afterward said, that if he had known it was a burial he would
not have allowed any firing in that direction." [1] The Judge is
the first writer to report that one hundred and fifty loyalist
prisoners were left to burn in the vessels deserted by the Americans at the time the British took forts Clinton and Montgomery
on the Hudson in 1777—an item which, had it been true, could
not have failed to be noticed at the time. The British reports
mention no such distressing episode of that expedition. In his
account of the Stony Point operations, the Judge charges the
loss of that post, when stormed by Wayne in 1779, upon the
neglect and convivialty of the commanding officer, Colonel

Johnson, who is stated to have been carousing at the time with a party of friends from the garrison at Verplank's Point. But Johnson's own brief report, the narrative of Admiral Collier, and statements of American officers show that the British were on the alert, and the Colonel at his post at least at the critical moment. Furthermore, the returns of prisoners taken give no officers other than those belonging to the Stony Point garrison, thus excluding the theory of a party from Verplank's. Again, when Lord Rawdon, the British officer who commanded in South Carolina after Cornwallis marched north, was made prisoner by the French fleet under de Grasse, and taken into the Chesapeake, Congress, according to the Judge, demanded his surrender to the American authorities. "Surprising to relate," he exclaims, "yet an absolute, undeniable fact! They had the impudence, or assurance, or rather both, to send a Committee on board the fleet, and demand of the Compte the delivery of his Lordship into their hands, that they might, as they declared, execute him by way of retaliation for the execution of Hayne [in Charleston!." De Grasse, however, we are informed, spurned the proposal, refused to surrender Rawdon and snubbed the Committee in a manner entirely gratifying to the Judge. We are to accept this as an "absolute, undeniable truth" on Judge Jones' *dictum* solely, for he gives no authority for the statement. The records, on the other hand, contain nothing tending to corroborate it, but rather authorize its denial. That Congress should send a Committee so long a distance on such an errand is wholly improbable upon its face. In the numerous documents relating to the Yorktown campaign, no mention is made of the presence at any time of such a Committee. Neither Washington, Rochambeau, La Fayette, Knox, Wayne and other officers, who leave journals and correspondence covering the siege operations, refer to the matter. The demand for Rawdon would have been a purely military act to be left to the Commander-in-Chief and not to Congress; and the demand, furthermore, would without doubt have passed through Rochambeau as the Commander of the French forces, but Rochambeau has not a word in his "Memoirs" about Rawdon, the demand or the refusal. The Judge's undeniable truth, not "surprising to relate," looks much like a fiction. One more topic in this connection, and that concerns some of the Judge's speculations in regard to the movements of Cornwallis in North Carolina in 1781. If the Judge was familiar with the published controversy between that General and Sir Henry Clinton respecting the former's campaign in the South and his final surrender, he fails to show it in the present instance. He claims that Cornwallis, upon becoming sensible of his inability to hold his own in North Carolina after the battle of Guilford Court House, should have retreated back to South Carolina and prepared for another campaign rather than march to Wilmington and afterwards to Virginia. But, says the Judge, "His Lordship, no doubt, *was following the orders of the Commander-in-Chief*, from which he had no right to deviate upon any contingency whatever." Now, had Judge Jones read Clinton's letters on the subject, published immediately after the war, he would have ascertained that Clinton's judgment in the case was identical with his own, and that the former was opposed to the march of Cornwallis northward after his operations in North Carolina. In his "Observations" on Stedman, the General says: " Perhaps Mr. Stedman does not know that Lord Cornwallis had been *ordered*, and had *promised*, in case of failure in North Carolina, to fall back on South Carolina, and secure it." It is evident that Judge Jones, also, did not know it, and that his personal hostility to Clinton prompted him to adopt any theory or supposition that would help to damage the General's reputation. To these minor misstatements (if they are of a minor order) still more might readily be added, were further illustration necessary.

As a natural conclusion to the foregoing criticisms and observations, the question occurs whether the important errors and the numerous lesser blunders to be found in Judge Jones' work do not form the basis of an unfavorable estimate of its value *as an authority*. It has been seen that the Judge makes most positive assertions which have no foundation in fact—that, though being a Judge, he gives currency to outrageous libels, the truth of which he could not have been assured of, for the single reason that they were false—that in many cases he draws unwarrantable inferences—that he shows the bitterness of his

pen by the readiness with which he seems to accept and perpetuate current slanders or falsehoods in regard to those whom
he wishes to expose—and that he writes much from hearsay or
irresponsible sources of information. At least these conclusions
appear to be authorized so far as they follow from and apply to
the cases examined. And if these are admissible as necessary
and correct conclusions—if, in a word, Judge Jones has, in the
cases noticed, proved himself a blundering and unreliable witness and writer, *what guarantee have we that he has given us
truth and accuracy in the many other statements which he pretends
to publish as secret history, but which, in the probable absence
of records, cannot be either substantiated or denied to-day?*
Suspicion at once attaches to his entire work. The Judge's
continued and pitiless references to William Smith, to Sir Henry
Clinton, to General Robertson, to Sir William Jay, to Ludlow
and Elliott—his pen-pictures of and insinuations in regard
to General Schuyler, Lord Sterling, Francis Lewis, McDougal,
John Morin Scott, William Livingston and other characters on
both sides—his opinions and impressions generally of men
and events, his exposition of motives, and his wholesale
denunciation of whomsoever and whatsoever affected a good and
true loyalist unfavorably—how far is the Judge to be followed
in these and similar effusions that characterize his narrative?
How much in it and precisely what is to be accepted, in view of
what, upon evidence, it is certain cannot be accepted? Where is
the line to be drawn between the Judge as an accurate historian
and the Judge as a libeller and credulous chronicler of report and
rumor? The question is raised legitimately. That Judge Jones'
work is to be rejected as entirely worthless is not a claim
advanced in this connection, but we submit whether the historical student, anxious to probe records to the bottom and welcom-
ing everything which has the "contemporary" mark upon it, can
include the Judge among his trustworthy informants. There
must remain a conviction that however true the Judge's statements may prove to be in any given case, *they still require
confirmation.*

www.ingramcontent.com/pod-product-compliance
Lightning Source LLC
Chambersburg PA
CBHW021423090426
42742CB00009B/1229